Yale Language Series

12 American Voices

An Authentic Listening and Integrated-Skills Textbook

Maurice Cogan Hauck with Kenneth MacDougall

Based on National Public Radio Documentaries by David Isay

YALE UNIVERSITY PRESS NEW HAVEN AND LONDON

Publisher: Mary Jane Peluso
Production Controller: Aldo Cupo
Editorial Assistant: Emily Saglimbeni
Designer: Rebecca Gibb
Set in Baskerville type by Integrated Publishing Solutions,
Grand Rapids, MI. Printed in the United States of America by Victor Graphics, Inc.

Library of Congress Cataloging-in-Publication Data

Hauck, Maurice Cogan, 1966–
        Twelve American voices : an authentic listening and integrated-skills textook /
    Maurice Cogan Hauck with Kenneth MacDougall.
            p.   cm.—(Yale language series)
        "Based on National Public Radio documentaries by David Isay."
        ISBN 0-300-08960-0 (alk. paper)
                1. English language—Textbooks for foreign speakers. 2. United States—Social life
    and customs—Problems, exercises, etc. 3. Listening—Problems, exercises, etc. 4. Readers—
    United States.   I. MacDougall, Kenneth, 1963–.   II. Isay, David.   III. Title.   IV. Series
    PE1128 .H39 2002
    428.3′4—dc21   2001016142

A catalogue record for this book is available from the British Library.

The paper in this book meets the guidelines for permanence and durability of the Committee on Production Guidelines for Book Longevity of the Council on Library Resources.

10 9 8 7 6 5 4 3 2 1

This book is dedicated to Marcia Cogan, Charlie Hauck,
John and Vera MacDougall, and to all the others
who have taught us through the years.

Contents

To the Instructor

Twelve American Voices is an ESOL textbook that uses the award-winning radio stories of National Public Radio contributor David Isay as a basis for listening and integrated-skills work. The book leads students to a holistic understanding of a series of culturally rich broadcasts about American traditions and unique individuals. In each chapter, contextualized vocabulary and language structure exercises help students analyze the language in the broadcasts, and a variety of discussion, writing, and project activities provide opportunities for them to express their reactions to the themes the broadcasts contain.

We decided to write *Twelve American Voices* because we had trouble finding authentic materials that college and adult students find genuinely interesting, materials that respect their intelligence and life experience and also provide an opportunity for focused language study. David Isay's radio stories, for which his honors include three Peabody Awards and a MacArthur "genius" grant, fill the bill perfectly. Designed to inform and entertain native speakers, they deal with traditions and changes in contemporary U.S. culture and address a range of topics, some lighthearted and some quite serious. Students are introduced to the world's only senior citizen disc-jockey team and to a woman who played a role in a historic civil rights sit-in. They meet a retired minister in the Pacific Northwest whose diary is approaching 35 million words, and also parents in the South Bronx who are struggling to control their crack-addicted daughter. In addition to learning about a very traditional purveyor of kosher wine for Passover, they drop in on a very unorthodox charity Santa Claus as he solicits donations on a street corner.

The people featured in these broadcasts speak a range of Englishes. In addition to David's narration, we hear the distinctly non-native (but highly communicative) voice of an immigrant Chinese businessman and the non-standard dialect of an African-American waitress, as well as a wide variety of speakers of more standard Englishes from different corners of American society.

Taken together, David's broadcasts give an intimate picture of what he calls the "poetry on the edges of society" and give students an opportunity to explore topics of real interest that are all too rarely addressed in ESOL textbooks.

Twelve American Voices is designed to be used in either ESL or EFL classrooms, whether students speak the same first language or have a range of mother tongues. It can be used as a primary textbook for a course focusing on listening and conversation or, along with a grammar text and a reader, can serve as one part of a complete language program.

Each chapter is self-contained, and the level of difficulty increases through the book, with Chapters 1 to 6 at an intermediate level and Chapters 7 to 12 at an upper-intermediate level. We have found, however, that each of these chapters can be used successfully with a range of levels as long as the tasks assigned, the amount of time allowed, and the degree of support offered are appropriate. Each chapter is designed to take approximately one hundred minutes of class time, exclusive of the project activity, which will generally require at least an entire class period.

The activities built around David's broadcasts are designed to give students both enough structure to understand the texts and also the freedom to explore the aspects they find most interesting. Each chapter concerns a single radio story and consists of the following elements.

Before Listening

Because learners are able to understand more when the context is known, an *Orientation* exercise asks students to relate some of the themes of the broadcast to their own experience. This arouses students' curiosity, activates their latent knowledge of the subject area, and makes the listening more realistic and meaningful.

A *Vocabulary* activity presents ten to fifteen key lexical items, with a focus on words central to understanding the world in which the story takes place.

Listening and Understanding

A three-part listening sequence leads students through progressively deeper and more native-like levels of understanding and appreciation of the broadcast.

Students begin by reading a brief *Introduction* that further contextualizes the broadcast. A *First Listening: Predicting* exercise provides a focus for students' initial exposure to the broadcast. Students then listen to check on their predictions and see how much they can understand of the broadcast.

In *Listening for Comprehension,* students are asked to demonstrate a fairly detailed literal understanding of the text. Items in this more intensive activity follow the chronology of the text and include both short-answer and more open-ended questions.

For the final listening, students can follow along with the tapescript as they work to complete the *Listening for Analysis* activity. Here we encourage students to develop their own interpretation of the broadcasts as they analyze how it creates its meanings.

Additionally, two Language Focus activities look at points of language structure as they occur systematically in the text. *Language Focus A* addresses such discrete grammar topics as phrasal verbs and preposition use. Students are guided to understand the meaning and use of the particular feature and then are given a chance to practice it in a directed exercise. *Language Focus B* addresses broader issues of language, style, and culture. These include non-sexist language; the language of hype; and polite and impolite language. In each Language Focus B, students are given responsibility for analyzing the text and working out its meanings for themselves.

After Listening

At the end of each chapter a variety of thought-provoking discussion, writing, and fluency activities allow students to express their own feelings, associations, and opinions about the broadcast.

Discussion Activities encourage students to relate the themes of the broadcast to their own experiences and to explore what they and their classmates feel about the issues that have been raised.

Writing Activities offer a choice between responding personally to the broadcast or relating its themes to cultural values in the United States or the students' home countries. Students are asked to write in a range of genres— personal narrative, academic essay, personal and business letters, etc.

Each chapter ends with a *Project Activity* of a different type—research activity, debate, roleplay, etc.—which offers an opportunity to go beyond the broadcast itself in exploring the themes presented. Some projects can be conducted within the confines of the school (e.g., students producing their own TV talk show). Other projects call on students to leave the classroom and interact with the larger community (e.g., doing research on the Civil Rights Movement or conducting a survey on uses of writing).

A more detailed explanation of the methodology, along with teaching suggestions and culture and language notes for each chapter, can be found in the accompanying *Instructor's Manual*.

David Isay's broadcasts have been a source of real pleasure and insight in our classrooms, and we are excited to share them with the ESOL community. We hope that you and your students will find both the broadcasts and the lessons enjoyable and interesting. And we hope that *Twelve American Voices* will help prepare your students to enter the broad and inclusive speech community of American English.

To the Student

We have written this book for a simple reason. We feel that the best way for students to improve their English, and to explore American culture, is to work with the same kinds of materials that we ourselves enjoy. We are excited to share David Isay's radio documentaries with you because we have found them valuable and interesting enough to listen to again and again.

David Isay is a reporter who is truly passionate about his work. He has dedicated his career to telling stories from the corners of American society, giving a voice to people who are rarely noticed. We hope that some of his passion will rub off on you and that you will find yourself listening not only to learn the language but also because you want to understand and respond to the broadcasts. In fact, the best language learning will happen when you forget that you are studying and find yourself simply using English to communicate.

The broadcasts in *Twelve American Voices* have not been simplified or edited for English learners; they are in exactly the same form as they appeared on the radio. (That is what is meant by the word "authentic" in the book's subtitle.) Authentic radio broadcasts can be more interesting than other types of listening materials, but they can also be more challenging. There is no control over the number of unfamiliar words and expressions that they contain. For this reason it is not necessary to understand absolutely every word in a broadcast. You are learning well as long as you are able to respond intelligently to the story, asking questions and expressing your own opinion about those things that interest you.

Beyond simply understanding the broadcasts that it contains, *Twelve American Voices* is also designed to help you develop into a more skilled listener, one capable of listening more effectively on your own. You will be asked to pay close attention to your own listening process and to get used to asking such questions as "What have I understood so far?" "What do I think of what I've heard?" "What more would I like to find out?" and "What in my own life or experience does this connect to?" This kind of active listening is important to improving your communicative skills.

Many activities in this book involve working with a partner or in a group. This is because you can learn a great deal by sharing your ideas, reactions, and interpretations. For one thing, you will come to realize how much of the broadcast you and your classmates can work out together, without turning to your instructor or a dictionary for help. More important, learning to work out meanings will make you better able to teach yourself to communicate in English.

If you are using this book for self-study rather than as part of a class it will be more difficult to do the group activities. Still, it makes sense to share this book and your reactions with someone else who speaks English or is studying it. For more information, see the *Instructor's Manual*, which has explanations of many of the exercises and notes on some of the language and the cultural background of the broadcasts.

Welcome to *Twelve American Voices*. We hope that you enjoy working with it as much as we enjoyed writing it. We wish you every success in your studies.

Acknowledgments

A great many people have helped us on the long journey of writing this book.

First of all, we would like to thank David Isay and photographer Harvey Wang for creating such a wonderful body of work and for their generosity in sharing it with us and our students.

We also are deeply grateful to Sheryl Olinsky for bringing us into the world of publishing and to Mary Jane Peluso for taking us in at Yale University Press and supporting us in bringing the spirit of David's stories into the classroom. Thanks also to Ellen Ciosek, Heidi Downey, Jill Sarkady, and the entire staff of Yale University Press. We would also like to thank our agent, Jonathan Dolger, for sticking with us throughout this process.

Appreciation is due faculty members at Teachers College, Columbia University, who contributed advice and support: Clifford Hill, Franklin Horowitz, JoAnne Kleifgen, Eric Larsen, and Carol Numrich. It is difficult to imagine how this book could have been produced without the staff of the TC computer labs, particularly the consultants in 242 Horace Mann and 345 Macy Hall.

Our work also benefited from the input of colleagues and students at the institutions where we have taught previous versions of this book: Language Studies International, Berkeley; St. Giles College, San Francisco; Baruch College, CUNY; English International, San Francisco; the Hunter College International English Language Institute, CUNY; Language Resources, Kobe; Lehman College, CUNY; Fudan University, Shanghai; and the UC Berkeley Summer Writing Programs.

A number of people piloted or reviewed early versions of these lessons. We would like to thank Kate Baldus, Annice Barber, Clinton Boswell, Lincoln Davis, Aleksander Dietrichson, Gabrielle Goodwin, Erik Gundersen, John Hoffsis, Ruskin Hunt, Sharon Jones, Barbara Kaiser, Irene Koshik, Daniela Liese, Elizabeth Jean Meddeb, Roosevelt Montás, Annie Mullen, Leslie Nabors, Itsuko Nakamura, Willie Nelson, Helen Parker, Caleb Paull, Josie Piraino, Melissa Reeve, Ed Scarrey, Shira Seaman, Maggie Sokolik, Brandon Spars, Margie Wald, Abigail Ward, Dale Ward, and Belinda Yanda. We would also like to thank the following reviewers for their close reading and helpful comments: Kurt Belgum, Georgia Institute of Technology; Patricia Harris, Texas A&M University; Brenda Imber, University of Michigan; and Susan Vik, Boston University. We thank, as well, Sister Kathleen Feeley, S.S.N.D., for her prayers.

Finally, Maurice would like to thank Alexandra Klein for support and inspiration at crucial stages, and Ken would especially like to thank Therese Naber for all of her support.

"David leads me to the big round table in the middle of the restaurant. A table which, like many others, holds memories for me."

Photo by Claudette Buelow

1 Hunan Chef

Before Listening

ORIENTATION

Tell your group about a "regular" restaurant you used to go to. First, describe the restaurant. For example, tell your group about the type of food, the atmosphere, and the prices. Then explain why it was the right place for you. How do you feel when you think about it now?

When you are finished, your group will have a chance to share what you discussed with the class.

VOCABULARY

The following words and phrases all have to do with restaurants. Which of them do you already know? Work with your group to fill in the appropriate word from the box on the line after each definition. If no one in your group can find the answer, you may use a dictionary. The first one has been done for you as an example.

sip	diced
leftovers	savor
complimentary	to settle the bill
carafe	to pick up the tab
sliced	to pay the check
famished	

1. an *adjective* that means, "very hungry, almost starving." *famished*

2. a *verb* that means "eat slowly and really enjoy the taste."

_____

3. a *noun* that refers to something that you can serve wine in.

_____

4. two *verbs* that describe ways meat or vegetables can be cut.

_____ ; _____

5. an *adjective* that means "free" or "on the house"; you don't have to pay for it.

_____

6. a *noun* that refers to food which will be saved and eaten on another day.

_____

7. a *verb* that means to drink slowly or in small amounts. _____

8. two phrases that mean to pay for your meal. _____ ;

_____

9. one phrase that means to pay for someone else's meal. _____

Listening and Understanding

INTRODUCTION

David Isay, the narrator of all of the broadcasts in this book, eats regularly at Hunan Chef, a small restaurant in his neighborhood. This broadcast was recorded one night when he called up for a delivery and got some bad news. In this story, David spends some time having dinner at Hunan Chef and sharing his memories of a place that has been like a home away from home for him.

FIRST LISTENING: PREDICTING

Before listening to the broadcast, predict what the answer to each of the following questions will be. Write your response on the lines provided.

1. What kind of food must Hunan Chef serve? _____

_____

2. Why might the restaurant be going out of business? _____

_____

3. How much do you think Crispy Orange Chicken probably costs?

_____

Listen to the broadcast to check the answers to your predictions. Don't worry about understanding everything in the story. You'll have a chance to hear it again.

LISTENING FOR COMPREHENSION

Read over the following questions and see whether there are any that you can answer from your first listening. Then listen to the broadcast again to check your answers and to find the answers to the remaining questions.

1. How long has David Isay been a regular customer at Hunan Chef?

_____

2. On what nights does he usually eat at the restaurant? _____

3. What did he do when he heard that the restaurant was closing?

_____

_____

4. What important news did David's best friend from college share with him at Hunan Chef?

_____

_____

5. What solution did the owner offer when David became worried about where he was going to eat?

_____

_____

6. According to David, how good was the food at Hunan Chef?

_____

_____

7. Was David ever disappointed with the food at Hunan Chef? Explain.

_____

_____

_____

8. How much did David pay for his last meal at Hunan Chef? Explain.

_____

_____

LANGUAGE FOCUS A: PHRASAL VERBS (1)

A phrasal verb is a special type of verb created by combining a verb and a preposition. Together they create a phrasal verb (also known as a "multiword verb") with a special meaning. The meaning of a phrasal verb might not be clear even if you know what each word means on its own. Note the following sentence.

David Isay used to *hang out* at Hunan Chef.

To "hang out" somewhere means to spend a lot of time there on a casual basis. However, you might not guess this meaning even if you knew the meaning of both "hang" and "out."

A. With a partner, read each of the following sentences. Note the italicized phrasal verb. Then find the definition that matches it. Write the letter next to the definition in the space provided. The first one has been done for you.

_____d_____ 1. David tried to *keep* his visits *down* to one a week.

_____ 2. Whenever he needed a comforting meal, he would *call up* Hunan Chef for a delivery.

_____ 3. When the owner *picked up*, David Isay was confused.

_____ 4. When David heard the news, he *threw on* a coat.

_____ 5. Then he *headed over* to Hunan Chef.

_____ 6. The rent hike *put* Hunan Chef *out of business*.

_____ 7. Only once in nine years did Hunan Chef *let* David *down*.

_____ 8. He was disappointed when an order of sliced chicken *showed up* at his apartment.

a. disappoint
b. answered the phone
c. make a telephone call
d. minimize
e. went
f. destroyed the business
g. arrived
h. put on rather quickly

B. Phrasal verbs can often replace more formal sounding verbs. For example, it sounds less formal for David Isay to say that he was *let down* by his delivery than to say that he was *disappointed*. (Because they are generally informal, phrasal verbs are used more often in speaking than in writing.)

Each of the following pairs of sentences has a formal version on the left and an informal version on the right. Complete each informal sentence with one of the prepositions in the box below to form a phrasal verb so that it means the same thing as the sentence on the left.

up / down
in / out
on / off

1. At what time did you awaken this morning?
   When did you get _____ ?

2. I am very tired and will now retire to bed.
   I'm beat so I think I'm going to turn _____ .

3. She phoned to say she's been delayed at the office.
   She called to say she's been held _____ at work.

4. Please lower the volume of your radio.
   Could you turn your radio _____ ?

5. I suspect that that story is an invention.
   I think the story was probably made _____ .

6. What was the conclusion of the film?
   How did the movie turn _____ ?

7. I hope they will move more quickly.
   I hope they will hurry _____ .

8. Please wait a moment.
   Can you hold _____ for just a minute?

9. You must register by the 3rd of September.
   You need to sign _____ by September 3rd.

10. The meeting has been postponed until Tuesday.
    The meeting is being put _____ until Tuesday.

LISTENING FOR ANALYSIS

Listen to the broadcast again for answers to the following questions. As you listen, follow along with the transcript and mark all the passages that help you answer the questions. Write your answers to the questions on the lines provided. You may also mark any places where the meaning of the story is unclear and ask your teacher for an explanation.

Look over the following questions before listening to the story for a final time.

1. How would you describe David Isay? (Consider his actions. They point to the kind of person he is.)

_____

_____

_____

2. How would you describe David Ma, the owner of Hunan chef?

_____

_____

_____

3. Why do you think Hunan Chef was so special to David Isay?

_____

_____

_____

4. Is this a sad story or a happy one? Could it be both? Explain your reaction.

_____

_____

_____

_____

LANGUAGE FOCUS B: VOCABULARY IN CONTEXT (1)

When you encounter an unfamiliar word, you can use context clues—the words or sentences before and after it—to help you figure out its meaning. For example, in the following sentence you can use context clues to figure out the meaning of the italicized word.

> I've eaten at Hunan Chef *religiously* since the first week of my freshman year at college, nearly nine years ago. Usually I'm only at the restaurant on Monday nights. I try to keep my visits down to one a week.

We can see from the second sentence that David Isay eats at Hunan Chef every week, usually on the same day. This lets us know that the word *religiously* means something like "regularly; on a fixed schedule or in a very reliable way."

Find each of the following words or phrases in the tapescript (the line number is given). Use the context clues to help you figure out what each one means. Then find the definition for the word or phrase and write the appropriate letter in the space provided. The first one has been done for you.

____g____ 1. reminisce (line 36)

_____ 2. hike (line 38)

_____ 3. identical (line 56)

_____ 4. outstanding (line 58)

_____ 5. consistent (line 58)

_____ 6. tendency (line 60)

_____ 7. committed . . . to memory (lines 71–72)

_____ 8. keepsake memento (line 88)

    a. exactly alike
    b. better than the others
    c. increase or raise

d. memorized

e. a thing that helps you to remember the past

f. a preference for doing something

g. talk about times in the past

h. reliable, always the same

After Listening

DISCUSSION ACTIVITIES

With your group, choose one of the following activities.

A. There's a saying in English, "There's no such thing as a free lunch." What does this saying mean? Do you agree with this idea? Explain your opinion, relating this saying to the broadcast.

B. Think about a friend of yours with a very different background from your own. This person could be someone from another country or someone who is different from you in another way. Tell your group about your friend. What was the basis of your friendship? Explain how the differences affected your relationship, either positively or negatively.

WRITING ACTIVITIES

Choose one of the following topics.

A. Think of a place that was once a "home away from home" for you the way that Hunan Chef was for David Isay. Write the story of something that happened to you there. It could be a sad story, such as the last time you visited the place, or it could be a fond memory. Try to use specific details in order to give the reader a clear sense of what the place was like and what it meant to you.

B. Write a review of a restaurant you ate at recently. Would you recommend this restaurant to others? Explain why or why not. In your review, be sure to include information about the quality of the food, the friendliness and efficiency of the staff, the atmosphere, and the prices.

PROJECT ACTIVITY: PLANNING YOUR OWN RESTAURANT

Imagine that you have decided to quit your job and open a restaurant. The other members of your group will be your partners. Together make a plan for your new business. You will need to consider the following questions:

1. Where will your restaurant be located?
2. What kind of food will it serve?
3. What will the prices be like? (You may want to design a menu.)
4. What will the atmosphere be like?
5. Most important, what will be special about your restaurant? Why will people who have eaten there once want to come back again?

When you are ready, present your plans for the restaurant to the class.

"We call ourselves the last resort. This is it. I mean, if we can't figure out where your letter was supposed to go, that's it. We consider ourselves the best."

Photo by Claudette Buelow

2 The Nixie Clerk

Before Listening

ORIENTATION

Read over the following list of services. Put a check in front of each one that you think is provided by the U.S. Postal Service.

_____1. Get packaging to send a parcel.

_____2. Pay a utility bill.

_____3. Send an overnight package.

_____4. Get information about wanted criminals.

_____5. Buy a money order.

_____6. Register for the Selective Service (in case of a military draft).

_____7. Get tax forms.

_____8. Make a long-distance phone call.

Check your answers with your teacher and then discuss the following question: How is the U.S. Postal Service different from the post office in your home country?

VOCABULARY

In the following drawing, identify each of the following parts of a letter. Write the correct number in the space provided.

1. envelope
2. the return address
3. the mailing address:
   a. addressee
   b. street address
   c. zip code
4. the stamp or postage
5. the postmark

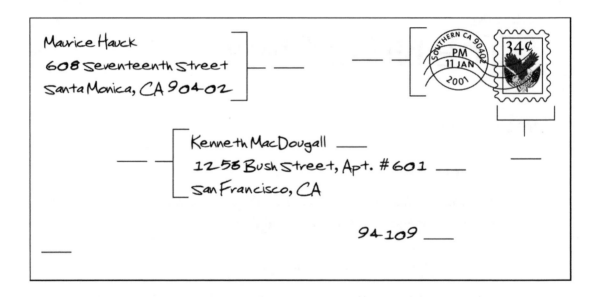

Check your work with a partner. Then discuss the following question: What is the purpose of each part—for example, why is a return address included?

Listening and Understanding

INTRODUCTION

Have you ever received a letter, looked at the badly written address on the envelope and wondered how it ever found its way to you? Well, David Isay decided to find out. He visited the Morgan Central Mail Facility, a major sorting center for the U.S. Postal Service, to find out how the post office deals with hard-to-read envelopes.

FIRST LISTENING: PREDICTING

What do you think the U.S. Postal Service does with envelopes that are hard to read? Write your response on the lines provided. _____

_____

_____

Listen to the story to check the answer to your prediction. Don't worry about understanding everything in the story. You'll have a chance to hear it again.

LISTENING FOR COMPREHENSION

Read over the following questions and see whether there are any that you can answer from your first listening. Then listen to the broadcast again to check your answers and to find the answers to the remaining questions.

1. Describe the room in which the mail is sorted. _____

_____

_____

2. How do the nixie clerks get the envelopes they will need to work on?

_____

_____

3. Does Al Flynn have trouble reading most envelopes?

_____

_____

4. What are some of the strange things that Al finds on envelopes?

_____

_____

5. Which of the following actions does Al take when he is working on a "toughie"? Put a check in front of each one.

_____ a. Stands very still.

_____ b. Asks a coworker for help.

_____ c. Matches letters.

_____ d. Sounds it out.

_____ e. Uses a computer scanner.

6. What happens to letters when the nixie clerks are not successful?

_____

_____

7. How many letters does Al work on during an average shift?

_____

8. How does Al feel at the end of his workday?

_____

_____

LANGUAGE FOCUS A: NONSEXIST LANGUAGE

As women have taken on a wider range of roles in society, the language has changed to reflect the increasing level of equality between men and women. For example, a postal worker who delivers mail was traditionally referred to as a *mailman*. However, as more woman have taken on this work, the title for this job is now *mail carrier*.

A. For each of the traditional job titles in the left-hand column, try to come up with a word that can refer to both men and women. The best way to do that is usually to find a word that emphasizes the work that is done rather than the gender of the person doing it. Sometimes there is more than one possible answer. The first one has been done for you as an example.

1. policeman _police officer_   3. fireman _____

2. stewardess _____   4. salesman _____

5. cleaning lady_____   7. housewife_____

6. chairman_____   8. businessman _____

B. Identify the instance of sexism in each of the following sentences and then rewrite each sentence in a nonsexist way. In some cases there is more than one way to revise the sentence.

1. Every man has a responsibility to contribute to society. _____

_____

2. This new tax policy is intended to help the working man.

_____

_____

3. Jim and Sally got married yesterday, so they are no longer boyfriend and girlfriend, they are now man and wife.

_____

_____

_____

4. War has been a problem throughout the history of mankind.

_____

_____

5. Every student should try to do his best. _____

_____

_____

6. When a reporter covers a controversy, he has a responsibility to be fair to all sides.

_____

_____

_____

LISTENING FOR ANALYSIS

Below are listed four qualities that help make Al good at his job. As you listen to the story again, follow along with the transcript and mark the passage or passages that show each of these qualities. (You can also mark any places where the meaning of the story is unclear and ask your teacher for an explanation.)

1. He finds his job challenging.
2. He takes pride in doing a good job.
3. He gets excited when he succeeds.
4. He has a sense of humor about his work.

Share your work with a partner. Show your partner which parts of the transcript you marked and explain how they show that Al has each quality.

LANGUAGE FOCUS B: DESCRIBING A PROCESS WITH VIVID SIMPLE PRESENT VERBS

David Isay often uses the simple present tense to describe actions that Al Flynn and the other post office workers do over and over again, every day. By using precise, vivid verbs, David helps listeners to visualize the actions clearly. In the following description, note the italicized verbs that David uses to "paint a picture" of the process of sorting letters.

Sixty times a minute, a robotic vacuum arm *sucks up* a letter and *slaps* it in front of the clerks, who *punch* a button on the keyboard which *shoots* the letters into the appropriate zip code bins.

A. Underline each of the simple present verbs in the two following passages, which describe how Al Flynn works.

He simply draws a line under the offending scrawl, rewrites it to the side, and whisks it into the appropriate mail slot for delivery.

He holds the envelope up and freezes, staring at it motionlessly. Then he scratches his chin, makes a face, and massages his head.

B. Think of an action you do habitually. It could be part of your work or school day, or it could be something that you like to do in your free time, such as working in your garden or playing a sport. Write a brief paragraph in which you describe it as fully as possible. Use at least four vivid verbs in the simple present tense so that the reader can clearly visualize the action.

After Listening

DISCUSSION ACTIVITY

Al Flynn seems to have a job that suits him very well. What would be the perfect job for you? With your group, discuss your responses to each of the following questions.

1. What hours would you work? Would you have a regular schedule or would you work on a more flexible basis?

2. Al Flynn works by himself and doesn't talk to many people. Would you like this or would you need more human contact?

3. Where would you work? In an office? Outdoors? Would you like to do a lot of traveling? Would you like to telecommute (work from home using a computer, fax machine, and telephone)?

4. Would you rather be self-employed or work for a company? What are the advantages and disadvantages of each kind of job?

Now that you know what your perfect job would be like, discuss how you can go about getting it.

WRITING ACTIVITY

Choose one of the following topics. Ask your teacher or check with a writing handbook if you have any questions about the usual form of a business letter or a personal letter.

A. Write a cover letter (see note below) for your ideal job. It should fit on one page, and the paragraphs should be arranged as follows.

Paragraph 1: Identify the job you are applying for.

Paragraph 2: Explain how you are qualified for the job, and why it is the right job for you. (You can use some of the ideas from the discussion activity.)

Paragraph 3: Let the prospective employers know how they can reach you or how you will contact them for an interview.

Remember that business letters are usually typed. If you do write by hand, make sure that your writing is legible so that it doesn't end up going to a nixie clerk.

Cover Letters

When you apply for a job, you usually submit a resume, which is a summary of your personal information, education, and previous work experience. Along with your resume, you send a cover letter, in which you introduce yourself and express your interest in the job.

B. Write a personal letter. This letter can be addressed to someone you know who speaks English, describing what has been going on in your life in recent days (for example, since you started the class in which you are using this book). Or you could choose to write a letter to Al Flynn (or any of the other people interviewed in this book) about what you found interesting about his story and asking him any questions that come to mind.

Project Activity: Researching Your Ideal Job

Find a person who has a job that you find interesting. It can be a job in a field that you would like to enter or simply a job that you would like to know more about. Interview this person about the kind of work he or she does. You can use the following questions, or you can make up your own.

1. What is an average day like for you?
2. What do you like most about your job?
3. What do you like the least?
4. What do you find the most challenging?
5. Overall, do you find your job satisfying?
6. How long do you think you will stay in your job?

Take notes on what the person says and ask any follow-up questions that will help you to understand the job more fully. Report what you learn to the class.

"I actually talk to the ashes and I have a feeling for them. It's a ritual of life and death. I'm alive and they're gone! And that's what makes it interesting."

Photo by Harvey Wang

3 Airplane Ashes

Before Listening

ORIENTATION

With your group, choose one of the following activities.

A. Discuss your response to the following questions. What do you think happens to a person after he or she dies? Do you believe in reincarnation—life after death? Does your religion have teachings about this? What do you believe personally?

B. Tell your group about a funeral you once attended. How was the ceremony conducted? Who spoke? Was the body on view? How did the experience make you feel?

VOCABULARY

Most of the words in the box below relate to the topic of death. Look over the words, and then, with a partner, answer the following questions. You may use a dictionary if you wish. Write one word on each line provided. (Some of the words are used more than once.)

cremation	funeral
mourners	urn
burial	pilot
casket	oatmeal box

1. Which words describe a ceremony or ritual?

    a. _____

    b. _____

    c. _____

2. Which words describe a container?

    a. _____

    b. _____

    c. _____

3. Which words describe a person (or people)?

    a. _____

    b. _____

4. Which words really don't seem to fit into this category at all?

    a. _____

    b. _____

Listening and Understanding

INTRODUCTION

You are going to hear a story about Dick Falk, a man who runs an unusual funeral service called Airplane Ashes. Look at the photograph of Dick Falk on page 20. A person who runs a funeral business normally is called an "undertaker," but Dick Falk refers to himself as an "overtaker." What do you think he could mean by this word?

FIRST LISTENING: PREDICTING

Write your responses to the following questions on the lines provided.

1. How do you think Airplane Ashes will be different from a typical funeral service? Mention as many differences as possible.

_____

_____

_____

2. What do you think Dick Falk uses the oatmeal box for? _____

_____

_____

Listen to the broadcast to check on the answers to your predictions. Don't worry about understanding everything in the story. You'll have a chance to hear it again.

LISTENING FOR COMPREHENSION

Read over the following questions and see whether there are any you can answer from your first listening. Then listen to the broadcast again to check your answers and to find the answers to the remaining questions.

1. What is Dick Falk's nickname? Does it fit his personality?

_____

_____

2. According to Dick Falk, what are the advantages of an Airplane Ashes funeral?

_____

_____

3. How do the ashes get to Dick Falk? _____

_____

4. What do you know about the person whose ashes Dick is scattering today? Fill in the information on the lid of the oatmeal box below.

name _____
occupation _____
hometown _____
age at time of death _____
destination- _____
(the place where her ashes will be scattered)

5. What do the ashes look like? _____

6. How much does Dick Falk charge for his service? _____

7. Is Dick Falk's business doing well? Explain. _____

_____

_____

8. Where does Dick Falk want his own ashes to be scattered?

_____

_____

LANGUAGE FOCUS A: PARTS OF THE BODY USED AS VERBS

Nouns that refer to parts of the body (for example, "head," "nose," and "mouth") can often be used as verbs. For example, note the use of the noun "headed" as a verb in the following sentence from the broadcast.

Now she's *headed* towards the Statue of Liberty.

In the sentence above, "headed" means "traveling in a certain direction." Usually, such "body-part" verbs express actions that are associated with those parts of the body. (One "heads" in the direction one's head is facing.)

Read each of the following sentences and put the correct form of one of the body-part words from the box below into the blank. The meaning that the word should have is given in parentheses. Use each word only once. The first one has been done for you.

nose	elbow
hand	mouth
eye	shoulder
thumb	foot

1. Could you _____**hand**_____ me the newspaper under your chair, please?

   (to pass)

2. The crowd was very thick but she managed to _____ her way

   to the front. (to force one's way through other people)

3. Last night I _____ through that magazine, but didn't see the

   article you wanted me to read. (to turn pages)

4. It was a business lunch, so the company was _____ the bill.

   (to pay for)

5. I got furious when I found out that my little sister had been _____ about in my room while I was at school. (to explore a place where one is not allowed)

6. He ordered the vegetable plate because of his diet, but couldn't help _____ his wife's steak enviously. (to look at)

7. Although it was her boss's fault, the young executive had to _____ the blame for the disaster. (to take responsibility)

8. Because he was self-conscious about his singing voice, he only _____ the words to the hymns. (to pretend to speak or sing)

LISTENING FOR ANALYSIS

Dick Falk is something of an eccentric, a person who often does things in an unusual or odd way. For one thing, he runs an unusual business. In addition, he often speaks in a somewhat eccentric way. For example, consider how he explains the disadvantages of cremation.

> Every now and then, an urn will fall down and break and
> the ashes go all over the floor. Now you don't want to
> pick up your husband in a vacuum cleaner, which you'd
> have to do because you'd never get it out of the rug.

Listen as your teacher plays this part of the broadcast. Then answer the following questions. Write your responses on the lines provided.

1. How is Dick Falk's way of speaking about death different from the way most people speak about this topic?

_____

_____

_____

2. Does Dick Falk seem eccentric because of *what* he says, because of *how* he says it, or both? Explain.

_____

_____

_____

As you listen to the broadcast a final time, follow along with the transcript and mark the other places that reveal Dick Falk's eccentricity. (You can also mark any places where the meaning of the story is unclear and ask your teacher for an explanation.)

LANGUAGE FOCUS B: SEQUENCE WORDS

Sequence words such as "first," "then," and "next" are often used when telling a story to help the reader or listener keep track of the order in which events occurred.

A. The following extract from the story describes part of Dick Falk's ritual for scattering ashes. Read the extract over and notice each of the italicized words. Then answer the questions below.

> *First* the crematorium sends the ashes to his Forty-Second Street office. [. . .] *Then* he carefully transfers the ashes from the cremator's plain packaging to a more suitable receptacle.
> "*Actually*, I put them in what is known as an oatmeal box because it fits."
> *Then,* on to the top of this box, Falk scrawls the deceased client's name and vital information: his or her one-time profession, age at the time of death, hometown. _____ Falk rents a plane and a pilot, and off they go.

1. Of the italicized words, which one is not a sequence word? What idea does that word express?

_____

_____

2. Two of the words below could go into the blank in the last sentence of the extract and two could not. Put a check next to the words which could be used.

_____ a. first

_____ b. then

_____ c. finally

_____ d. actually

B. The paragraph below describes the first day at a language school. Read it over and put one of the following sequence words into each blank.

in the afternoon	next
finally	actually
first	then

There is a lot to get done on the first day of a term at a language school. a. _____, the students arrive at the school and gather in the auditorium. b. _____, the director gives a short introduction to the school and describes the schedule for the day. c. _____ tests of language ability are given. After that, everybody has lunch. d. _____, the teachers don't get much of a break because they have to mark the tests and put the students into the appropriate levels. e. _____, the students return to the school to learn what level they are in. f. _____, the director thanks the students for coming and reminds them to be on time for their classes the next morning.

C. Think of an event in your life that, like Dick Falk's ritual, takes place in a specific order (for example, what you do every morning before work or school or how you connect to the internet from your computer). Write a paragraph in which you explain your ritual in step-by-step detail. Use some of the sequence words from this exercise.

After Listening

DISCUSSION ACTIVITIES

With your group, choose one of the following activities.

A. Discuss the following questions. What would you want your own funeral to be like? Who would be there? Who would you want to give the eulogy (a speech remembering your life)? Would you want people to bring flowers or to make a donation to charity in your name? What do your wishes reveal about the type of person you are?

B. An Airplane Ashes funeral is a very nontraditional way to observe a death. What are the advantages of holding on to traditions (for example, traditional funerals)? What are the advantages of doing things in new or different ways? Do you like the idea of Airplane Ashes? Explain your opinion.

WRITING ACTIVITIES

Choose one of the following activities.

A. Write your will. (A will is a legal document that is read in the event of your death. It expresses your wishes for handling your possessions after you are gone.) You may approach this activity seriously, by writing about your true wishes, or you may give a humorous response (for example, what would you want to leave to each member of your English class?). Begin your will with the following phrase: "I, [your name], being of sound mind and body, declare . . . "

B. Think about a ritual in your home country that others might find interesting. (It could be a ritual for observing death, or it could be something unrelated to this story.) Write about this ritual in two ways. First, describe it so that a person who has never visited your country could understand it. Then, explain what this ritual shows about your country's culture and values.

PROJECT ACTIVITY: RESEARCHING AN UNUSUAL BUSINESS

David Isay found out about Airplane Ashes when he was thumbing through the yellow pages and saw Dick Falk's advertisement. Look through the yellow pages of the phone book in your community and choose an ad for a business or service that you find unusual or interesting. Call up the business and ask for an explanation of what the business is and how it works. Get information about what is done, how much it costs, etc. Report to the class on what you find.

"There's not a family in the world that loves their daughter any more than these people love their daughter. This was love. This was love and desperation."

Photo Courtesy Emily J. Saglimbeni

4 Chained Girl

Before Listening

ORIENTATION

With your group, read the proverb below and discuss the questions which follow.

> "Spare the rod and spoil the child."

1. What do you think this proverb means?
2. Do you agree with the idea it expresses? Why or why not?
3. When do you think physical punishment of a child *is* appropriate? When is it *not* appropriate?
4. Should the government have a role in deciding how parents are allowed to discipline their children? Explain your opinion.

VOCABULARY

With a partner, read each of the following sentences. Note the italicized word. Then find the definition for the word. Write the letter next to the definition in the space provided. The first one has been done for you.

_____i_____ 1. The two young boys *chained* their bikes to a lamppost before going into the mall.

_____ 2. After he was caught breaking into a grocery store, the thief was *arrested* and taken to jail.

_____ 3. When she started using drugs, she didn't worry about becoming an *addict*. She was sure that she would be able to quit at any time.

_____ 4. The prisoner walked slowly down the hallway because his ankles were *shackled*.

_____ 5. Some say that our legal system gives too much attention to criminals and does not respect the rights of crime *victims*.

_____ 6. It is the parents' responsibility to decide how to *punish* their children when they do something wrong.

_____ 7. A number of witnesses gave a detailed description of the *criminal* to the police.

_____ 8. After being found guilty the criminal was *imprisoned* for a period of two years.

_____ 9. The state troopers searched the nearby towns for the two men who had *escaped* from the prison in the middle of the night.

a. impose a penalty on one who has done something wrong
b. the people who suffer the results of crimes
c. connected with heavy chains so that one can't move easily
d. got away from a jail or some other confinement; made oneself free
e. a person with an uncontrollable need for something
f. put into jail for a long period
g. a person who has committed a crime
h. seized and taken into custody by the police
i. fastened with chains

Listening and Understanding

INTRODUCTION

In September 1991, there was a news report about a fifteen-year-old girl whose parents had chained her to a radiator in the living room of the family's apartment for two months. The girl had some freedom to move about the apartment and was given food and beverages, but she could not leave the apartment at all during that time. Eventually, a neighbor told the police about this situation, and the parents were arrested and taken to jail. Some of the headlines that appeared the next day are shown below.

FIRST LISTENING: PREDICTING

Based on what you have read above, what is your reaction to each of the following questions? Write your response on the lines provided.

1. What should be done with the girl who was chained? _____

_____

_____

2. What should be done to the parents of the girl? _____

_____

_____

3. What is your opinion of the neighbor who alerted the police? Did the neighbor do the right thing?

_____

_____

_____

Now listen to the broadcast. Don't worry about understanding all the details. Focus on listening to the main ideas.

After you have heard the broadcast, read over what you wrote in the Predicting activity. Have your answers to any of the questions changed? With a partner, discuss what you wrote before hearing the story and how you feel about it now.

LISTENING FOR COMPREHENSION

Read over the following questions and see if there are any you can answer from your first listening. Then listen to the broadcast again to check your answers and to find the answers to the remaining questions.

1. What kind of neighborhood do the Marreros live in? _____

_____

2. How old was Linda when her trouble began? What happened?

_____

_____

_____

3. What happened when the Marreros tried to get help from the city government?

_____

_____

_____

4. How much freedom did Linda have when she was chained? What was she able to do?

_____

_____

_____

5. What did the parents do with Linda when they had to leave the apartment?

_____

_____

_____

6. Did the Marreros get into trouble for chaining Linda? Explain what happened.

_____

_____

_____

7. What happened to Linda after her parents were forced to unchain her?

_____

_____

_____

8. What situation is Linda in at the end of the story?_____

_____

_____

LANGUAGE FOCUS A: PREPOSITION COMBINATIONS

Prepositions can be difficult to use correctly because there are often few clues for which is the right one for a given situation. Most prepositions, however, have a tendency to be used with certain nouns, verbs or adjectives. Each set of a noun, verb, or adjective plus the preposition it usually goes with can be called a preposition combination.

Prepositions can be difficult to use correctly because there are often few clues for which is the right one for a given situation. Most prepositions, however, typically are used with certain nouns, verbs, or adjectives. Each set of a noun, verb, or adjective plus the preposition it usually goes with can be called a "preposition combination." Note the verb plus preposition combination "keep from" in the following sentence.

> The Marreros wanted to *keep* their daughter *from* harm.

In some cases, a form of the verb "to be" is also part of the "verb plus preposition" combination.

Read the following sentences adapted from the broadcast and decide which preposition combination from the box fits into each blank space. You may need to change the form of some of the verbs. The first one has been done for you.

search for	be addicted to
worry about	be upset by
disappear from	grow angry with
prevent from	put [someone]
care for	through [some-
chain to	thing]
appeal to	

1. Maria and Eliezar Marrero were arrested for keeping their daughter Linda __chained to__ a radiator.

2. The Marreros _____ Linda's behavior when she started missing school and staying out late at night.

3. Linda's parents say she admitted that she _____ crack.

4. Their lives became one long _____ their daughter.

5. The Marreros say they _____ Linda's school, to the police, and to the city's child welfare agency for help, but were simply bounced back and forth.

6. Confidentiality _____ New York City's human resource administration _____ commenting on the case.

7. The troubling case quickly _____ the headlines but is still very much on the minds of many in the South Bronx.

8. The Marreros' community seems to be _____ increasingly _____ an overburdened social service system.

9. The Marreros say they simply wanted to _____ their daughter.

10. Roy Friberg thinks the system has abused the Marreros by _____ _____ them _____ so much difficulty.

11. Eliezar Jr. still feels that he has to _____ his sister.

LISTENING FOR ANALYSIS

As you listen to the story for a final time, follow along with the transcript. For each of the people listed below, identify the emotions you think they are feeling as they discuss Linda Marrero's situation. (These emotions might include sadness, anger, frustration, hopelessness, etc.) Write your responses on the lines provided.

1. Roy Friberg _____

_____

2. Eliezar Jr. _____

_____

3. Maria Marrero _____

_____

4. Eliezar Marrero _____

_____

As you listen, you can also mark any places where the meaning of the story is unclear and ask your teacher for an explanation. After you have given a response to each item, share your work with a partner.

LANGUAGE FOCUS B: FEATURES OF SPOKEN LANGUAGE

In spoken language, many of the words we use do not communicate content. Instead, they serve a function such as drawing attention to what we are going to say, stalling for time, or asking for agreement. (This is in contrast to writing, in which we usually use the most clear and concise language possible.)

For example, when Roy Friberg is talking about the neighbors' reaction to Linda being chained, he says,

> I mean, it was a very comfortable situation, you know what I mean?

A. With a partner, discuss the following questions about Roy's statement.

1. What part expresses the "content" of the sentence?
2. What function do the other parts of this sentence serve? (For example, what part attracts the listener's attention? What is the meaning of the last phrase?)
3. What are some of the things you say in your first language to perform these functions?
4. How would Roy's sentence be different if it were put into a more concise form that would be typical of written language?

B. With a partner, look over the tapescript for other examples of people speaking in a similar way. In each instance, rewrite their spoken language in a more concise way, focusing on the content of what the person was saying.

1. _____

_____

2. _____

_____

3. _____

_____

After Listening

DISCUSSION ACTIVITY

The story of the Marrero family is a very sad, even tragic one. But it is not very clear who is to blame for this situation. Who could be described as a criminal? Who could be described as a victim? Is there anyone who could be described as both?

With your group, rank each of the following people from 1 to 6 depending on how well you think they acted (1 is the best, 6 is the worst).

a. _____ Linda Marrero

b. _____ her parents

c. _____ the drug dealers

d. _____ the city agencies who did not help the Marreros

e. _____ the police who arrested the Marreros

f. _____ the neighbor who called the police

When you are ready, report your group's opinions to the class.

WRITING ACTIVITIES

Choose one of the following topics.

A. Roy Friberg says that the Marreros chained their daughter out of "love and desperation." Have you ever been desperate? Write about a time when you had to face a problem that you didn't feel able to solve. Explain what the problem was and how you dealt with it.

B. What role do you think the government should take in regulating how parents discipline their children? Should the government act to protect children, or should it not interfere in private family matters? Write an essay in which you express your opinion. Provide supporting evidence from your own experience, the experiences of others, or your reading.

PROJECT ACTIVITY: DEBATING HOW TO FIGHT ILLEGAL DRUGS

Your teacher will divide the class into two teams—Team A and Team B. The debate will focus on the following question: What is the best way to combat America's problem with illegal drugs?

GETTING READY

First, read the information in the appropriate box below and the procedures for the debate. Then, with the other members of your team, prepare for the debate. Decide who will speak and what arguments you will use. Think about how illegal drugs are handled in your home country and what you know about how they are handled in the United States. Consider what the other team's arguments are likely to be and how you can counter them.

Team A	**Team B**
The best way to fight illegal drugs is to reduce demand. There should be anti-drug education in the schools, and counseling and treatment should be available for people who have trouble with drugs. People who buy and use drugs are victims and should not be treated as criminals.	The only way to fight illegal drugs is to attack the supply by spending more money on border patrols and police pursuit of drug dealers. People who use drugs also are a big part of the problem. They should be given long prison sentences so that others will be discouraged from buying and using drugs.

PROCEDURE

Each team will begin with a three-minute opening statement. Flip a coin to see who gets to go first. Next, each debater will have an opportunity to ask a question of the other team. That team will have one minute to respond. Finally, each team will make a three-minute closing statement. Your teacher will act as timekeeper and will judge which team is the winner of the debate.

Photo by Claudette Buelow

"If you take one look at tonight's entertainment, in matching green and orange Hawaiian outfits loud enough to deafen, you'll know why this night will be different from all other nights."

5 Senior DJs

Before Listening

ORIENTATION

A. Complete each of the following sentences in your own words.

When I get old, . . .

1. . . . I hope I will _____

_____

2. . . . I expect I will _____

_____

3. . . . I fear I will _____

_____

With your group, compare your responses. What similarities do you find in the ways you view aging? What differences do you find?

B. Discuss your responses to the following questions with your group.

1. At what age do people retire in your home country?
2. What are some of the activities that people do when they are retired?
3. Tell your group about someone you know who is older, but "young at heart."

VOCABULARY

Read over the "age words" in the box below. With a partner, put them into the correct order in the left column of the chart and then write in the appropriate age range in the right column. Not all of the words are precise, and they may overlap in the range of years to which they refer. (One has been done for you as an example.)

adult	infant
adolescent	senior citizen
child	middle-aged person
toddler	

Age Word	Range of Years
adolescent	13 to 19

How does this relate to the words for age categories in your first language—do terms in your language cover the same ranges of years?

Listening and Understanding

INTRODUCTION

Estelle and Meyer Shurr claim to be the world's only professional husband-and-wife senior citizen disc-jockey team. For the past twenty years they've been providing entertainment for people who still want to dance to the music of the good old days. In this story, David Isay accompanies these two young-at-heart entertainers for an evening of dancing and socializing on the senior circuit.

FIRST LISTENING: PREDICTING

Before listening to the broadcast, write three questions that you hope the story will answer on the lines provided.

1. _____

_____

2. _____

_____

3. _____

_____

Now listen to the broadcast to see whether you can find the answers to your questions. Don't worry about understanding everything you hear. You'll have a chance to hear the story again.

LISTENING FOR COMPREHENSION

Read over the following questions and see whether there are any that you can answer from your first listening. Then listen to the broadcast again to check your answers and to find the answers to the remaining questions.

1. Where does tonight's dance take place? _____

_____

2. Who sets up the equipment? _____

_____

3. What inspired the Shurrs to become disc jockeys? _____

_____

4. Does tonight's dance get off to a good start? Explain. _____

_____

5. How does Meyer get people to keep dancing once they start?

_____

_____

6. What kind of equipment do the Shurrs use? _____

_____

7. What do the Shurrs think of today's pop music? Do they always agree?

_____

_____

8. Why do the Shurrs keep DJ-ing despite their health problems?

_____

_____

LANGUAGE FOCUS A: USING DESCRIPTIVE ADVERBS

An adverb is a word that modifies or describes a verb, an adjective, or another adverb. Usually an adverb is not grammatically required in a sentence, but it adds extra descriptive information that makes the sentence more expressive. Note the italicized adverb and the word it modifies in each of the following sentences.

> The DJ stopped the music *immediately*. (The adverb *immediately* modifies the verb "stopped.")

> They were *quite* happy to hear the old-fashioned music. (The adverb *quite* modifies the adjective "happy.")

> He arrived *very* late for the dance. (The adverb *very* modifies the adverb "late.")

An adverb can also modify an entire sentence.

> *Fortunately*, there were still tickets available when we arrived.

A. Note the italicized adverb in each of the sentences from the broadcast given below. Then find the definition for the adverb and write the letter next to the definition in the space provided. Identify which word (or words) in the sentence the adverb modifies. The first one has been done for you.

_____**d**_____ 1. The arriving seniors make their way *slowly* to one of the dozen tables. (The adverb *slowly* modifies the verb phrase "make their way.")

_____ 2. Club member Fritzie Levine *meticulously* lays out neat rows of dietetic cookies.

_____ 3. *Frequently*, the band didn't have a good rhythm.

_____ 4. Some members of the audience are tapping their fingers on the tables *impatiently*.

_____ 5. Others motion *wildly* for Estelle and Meyer to turn the volume down.

_____ 6. The Shurrs nod and wink at each other *knowingly*.

_____ 7. The Shurrs' act has a *distinctly* low-tech feel to it.

_____ 8. *Recently*, they've had to cut back their schedule to just a few shows per month.

a. with frustration, wanting something done more quickly
b. with very careful attention to detail
c. strong, easily perceived
d. not fast
e. at a time not long ago
f. often, on many occasions
g. in a way that shows shared understanding
h. with exaggerated, uncontrolled movements

B. Adverbs are often confused with adjectives, words which modify nouns. Adverbs are most often formed by adding the suffix "-ly" to the adjective form (although there are some irregular adverb forms, such as "very" and "quite" in Exercise A above). In each of the sentences below, choose the correct word, adjective or adverb, in parentheses.

1. I have a very (slow, slowly) computer so I can't use the newest software.
2. To avoid mistakes, it is important to do your work (slow, slowly) and (careful, carefully).
3. When we heard the news, my brother turned and gave me a (knowing, knowingly) smile.
4. I am a very (impatient, impatiently) person. I just can't pay attention long enough to proofread my papers as (meticulous, meticulously) as I should.
5. My sister speaks English very (good, well). Her pronunciation is particularly (good, well).

"Good" and "well"

The word "good" is most often used as an adjective in sentences such as "That is a good book." It can also be used as a different kind of adjective after a linking verb such as "feel." For example, we often say "I feel good" to express satisfaction with our physical or emotional condition. (In this use, "good" is called a predicate adjective.) You may also sometimes hear "good" used as an adverb in sentences such as "She can dance good." However, this use should be limited to informal conversation; it is not accepted in formal conversations or in writing.

The word "well" is most often used as an adverb, meaning "in a good way or manner" (for example, "My car runs well.") However, "well" can also be used as an adjective, as when it used to mean "healthy, not suffering from any sickness." (If a person is sick, we might send a card saying "Get well soon.")

LISTENING FOR ANALYSIS

The Shurrs are senior citizens, but through their work as disc jockeys they manage to remain young at heart. As you listen to the story for a final time, follow along with the transcript and complete the chart below. As you listen, you can also mark any places where the meaning of the story is unclear and ask your teacher for an explanation.

How do Estelle and Meyer Shurr show that . . .

. . . they are senior citizens?	. . . they remain "young at heart"?
1. They are "white haired and a little pudgy" and wear "thick glasses."	1. They carry in and set up the equipment themselves.
2.	2.
3.	3.
4.	4.

LANGUAGE FOCUS B: USING "WILL" AND "GOING TO"

Actions that will occur in the future can usually be expressed with either "will" or "going to" with little or no difference in meaning. For example, the following two sentences mean the same thing.

> I *will* retire when I turn sixty-five.

> I *am going to* retire when I turn sixty-five.

However, there are some situations in which only one of these forms can be used to express a certain meaning. Only "will" can be used to express a decision that is made at the moment of speaking (and expresses "willingness" to do something). In the following sentence from the broadcast, Estelle expresses her willingness to set up a piece of equipment.

I'*ll do* the microphone.

Only "going to" can be used to express a decision that has been made earlier (a "prior plan"). In the sentence below, the host of the seniors' party introduces the Shurrs, whose performance was arranged sometime before.

Tonight we'*re going to* have something a little different.

A. In the following sentences, fill in the appropriate form of "will" or "going to," plus a main verb. Note that a form of the verb "be" must be used before "going to." Because these sentences reflect spoken English, use the contracted forms of "will" and of "be." The first two have been done for you.

1. Those cases look heavy. I *'ll help* (help) you carry them up the stairs

2. Sorry, but I can't come over on Sunday. I *'m going to* help my friend John paint his living room. (in this case the speaker has previously made a plan to help John)

3. A: "Bad news, everybody. I just went into the kitchen and the fridge is empty. We need someone to go out and get some more beer."

   B: "I _____ (go). I need to pick up some cigarettes anyway."

4. A: "Hi, Janet. How do you like your dorm room?"

   B: "Actually, I'm having trouble sleeping. I'm on the first floor and it's kind of loud."

   C: "I _____ (switch) with you if you like. I don't mind moving because noise doesn't bother me much and in any case, I _____ (only be here) for two more nights."

5. A: "Do you have plans for New Year's Eve?"

   B: "Yes. I _____ (have dinner) with a group of friends, and then we _____ (go) to Times Square to watch the ball drop. How about you?"

   A: "I haven't made any plans. I don't really like crowds or big parties so I _____ (probably stay home)."

B. Each of the items below gives you a piece of news that you must decide how to react to. Use "will" to express the future in describing what you would do in each situation. The first one has been done for you.

1. You can't get home in time to watch your favorite TV show.

   I'll phone my roommate and ask her

   to tape it

2. Your company is having financial trouble and you've been asked to take a 20 percent pay cut.

   _____

   _____

3. A friend of yours tells you that he is moving into a new apartment on Friday and can't afford to pay for professional movers.

   _____

   _____

4. Your boyfriend or girlfriend decides to quit work and spend a year traveling around the world. He or she wants to go alone.

   _____

   _____

5. You have won $35 million in a lottery.

   _____

   _____

C. Now imagine that you plans are set and you are going to tell someone about the decision that you have made for each of the items above. Now that they are plans, use "going" to express your actions. The first one has been done for you.

1. I can't get home to watch my favorite TV show, so _I'm going to call my_ _roommate and ask her to tape it_ . (or, _"my roommate is_ _going to tape it for me."_)

2. My company asked me to take a 20 percent pay cut, so _____

_____ .

3. A friend of mine is moving into a new apartment on Friday and can't afford movers, so

_____

_____ .

4. My (boyfriend/girlfriend) has decided to travel around the world alone, so

_____

_____ .

5. I won $35 million in a lottery, so _____

_____ .

After Listening

DISCUSSION ACTIVITY

Do you have plans for your retirement? Below are four lifestyles that many retired people in the United States adopt. Read them over and decide which is the most attractive to you. Rank them from 1 to 4, with 1 being the most attractive and 4 the least. Explain your choices to your group.

1. _____ Move out of your home and spend your time traveling around the country in a big motor home with its own bedroom, living room, and kitchenette. (People who do this are called "snowbirds" because they usually go south for warm weather in the winter.)

2. _____ Continue living in your current home and keep active by playing golf or bridge and visiting other retired friends every day.

3. _____ Move to a new home closer to where your children live so that you can visit with them and see your grandchildren more often.

4. _____ Move into an "active living" complex for seniors, where there are many other retired people and organized social activities.

WRITING ACTIVITIES

Chose one of the following topics.

A. Write an essay describing an older person you admire.

B. Do you think people should be forced to retire from their jobs at age sixty-five? Write an essay in which you consider the benefits and disadvantages of this idea. Think about how such a policy would affect both individuals and the workplace as a whole. Support your opinion with examples and illustrations from your own experience, the experiences of others you know, or your reading.

PROJECT ACTIVITY: PREPARING FOR AN AGING POPULATION

The population of the United States today is rapidly aging. The biggest age group in the country—those born in the "baby boom" that followed World War II—will start to retire in the coming years.

With your group, come up with a plan for a public service program that will serve the needs of the enlarged senior population. Your program must be something that does not now exist and that will meet the needs of the aging baby boomers. For example, the Senior DJs meet a need by playing the kind of music older people enjoy dancing to. Identify another specific need of older people and then think about how you can most efficiently address that need.

When you are ready, each group will make a presentation to the rest of the class, which will act as the city council. The council members can ask any questions they would like and then vote on whether to fund your program.

"I don't want to sound like a ghoul, but it's a joy to try to capture as neatly and as gracefully as possible the essence of a special human being."

Photo by Claudette Buelow

6 Advance Obituaries

Before Listening

ORIENTATION

Read over the following questions and discuss your response with your group.

1. Do you usually read a newspaper in the morning? Which one? Briefly describe your paper and explain why you read it.

2. When you do read a newspaper, which of the following parts do you read? Circle the appropriate word. What does the way you read the newspaper reveal about you?

the front page	always	usually	sometimes	never
the sports	always	usually	sometimes	never
the comics	always	usually	sometimes	never
the business section	always	usually	sometimes	never
your horoscope	always	usually	sometimes	never

VOCABULARY

With a partner, read each of the following sentences. Note the italicized word. Then find the definition for the word. Write the letter next to the definition in the space provided. The first one has been done for you.

_____e_____ 1. Some say that to study history is the best preparation for a *journalist*.

_____ 2. The *newsroom* can be a loud and hectic place.

_____ 3. The *subject* of a story is not always pleased by the way it turns out.

_____ 4. Any journalist would love a chance to *interview* the president.

_____ 5. A *reporter* is responsible for presenting all sides of a controversial issue fairly.

_____ 6. Some people collect *clippings* of all the articles that mention them.

_____ 7. The *publisher* of a newspaper is a very powerful person.

_____ 8. Five p.m. is the *deadline* for stories that will appear in the morning edition of the next day's paper.

_____ 9. At the *morgue* you can find articles about a given subject that have been published in the past.

_____ 10. An *editor* must check articles both for content and for the quality of the writing.

a. the person who gathers information and writes a newspaper story

b. the person who a story is written about

c. the person who reviews the reporter's work and makes changes

d. the person who is in charge of a newspaper's business operations

e. a reporter, or any person, who researches, writes, edits, or presents the news

f. the time by which articles must be finished

g. the place in a newspaper office where writers and editors work

h. articles that have been cut out from newspapers and saved

i. to talk to a person in order to gather information from him or her

j. the place where old issues of the newspaper are stored

Listening and Understanding

INTRODUCTION

The *New York Times* is known as America's "paper of record" because what is written there will be referred to for years to come. In this story, David Isay visits the obituary writers, the reporters who write articles remembering the lives of well-known people who have died recently. Whatever they write will be an important monument to that person's life.

FIRST LISTENING: PREDICTING

Read over the following questions and write your responses on the lines provided.

1. What do you think an *advance* obituary could be? _____

_____

2. How do you think the advance obituary writers go about doing their job?

_____

_____

_____

Now listen to the broadcast to check on your predictions. Don't worry about understanding all the details. You will have a chance to hear the story again.

LISTENING FOR COMPREHENSION

Read over the following questions and see whether there are any you can answer from your first listening. Then listen to the broadcast again to check your answers and to find the answers to the remaining questions.

1. What is the atmosphere like in the *New York Times* newsroom? Is this how it was in the past?

_____

_____

2. Why does the *Times* prepare some obituaries before the "clients" die?

_____

_____

3. How does Peter Flint decide who he should write an advance obituary for?

_____

_____

4. What method does Marilyn Burger use to do research on her "clients"?

_____

_____

5. Why does Peter Flint prefer not to interview his clients directly?

_____

_____

6. Who is allowed to see their own advance obituary?

_____

_____

7. How does Peter Flint feel about his job?

_____

_____

8. What was Henry Fonda famous for? Give as detailed an answer as you can.

_____

_____

_____

LANGUAGE FOCUS A: PAST TENSE VERBS IN CONTEXT

When telling a story that takes place in the past, it's most common to use the simple past tense as the basic verb form. Other tenses will be used only when there is a need to express a different time idea.

A. Write the appropriate form of the given verb in each blank space in the passage below. Most of the verbs will be in the simple past. When a verb form other than simple past is needed, discuss what different time idea it expresses. A few of the verb forms are passives. The first one has been done for you.

Henry Fonda, who 1. __exemplified__ (*exemplify*) for nearly half a century a man of honesty and decency in more than one hundred films and stage plays, 2. _____ (*die*) early yesterday of chronic heart disease in Los Angeles. He 3. _____ (*be*) seventy-seven years old.

The actor, who 4. _____ (*retain*) a boyish candor and a gentle but firm manner, had long been a quintessential American hero. His image of a prairie Galahad 5. _____ (*enhance*) by his clean-cut features and firm jaw, tall, lean frame, and loping stride. His dry wit 6. _____ (*express*) in a distinctive middle-western twang.

Mr. Fonda 7._____ (*be*) a meticulous and modest craftsman, dedicated and intense, who thoroughly 8. _____ (*enjoy*) his profession. Mr. Fonda really 9. _____ (*live*) when he was acting and just 10. _____ (*exist*) when he wasn't. He 11. _____ (*remark*), "If I 12. _____ (*project*) anything of me into my roles, it's maybe a man with some dignity who 13. _____ (*try*) to be honest."

Besides his wife and children, he 14. _____ (*survive*) by four grandchildren and a sister, Harriet Warren of Omaha.

B. Interview a partner about the most important events of his or her life (birth, graduation[s], marriage, major accomplishments, etc.). Make a list of six to eight events and the time when each occurred. Then write an advance obituary for your partner, putting all the events into a paragraph. Because you are writing an obituary, you should use the past tense as your basic verb form.

LISTENING FOR ANALYSIS

Listen to the broadcast again to answer the following questions. As you listen, follow along with the transcript and underline passages that provide support for your responses. Write your responses on the lines provided. As you listen, you can also mark any places where the meaning of the story is unclear and ask your teacher for an explanation.

1. How would you describe Peter Flint's speaking style—is he interesting to listen to? Why or why not?

_____

_____

_____

2. How would you describe his writing style? What differences do you see between the way he speaks and the way he writes?

_____

_____

_____

3. Peter Flint says that part of his job is to "try to capture . . . the essence of a special human being." Do you think his obituary for Henry Fonda succeeds in doing this? Explain your opinion.

_____

_____

_____

LANGUAGE FOCUS B: USING THE PASSIVE VOICE

In a passive sentence the object of the active sentence becomes the subject of the passive sentence. When a verb is in the active voice, its subject performs the action. When a verb is in the passive voice, its subject is acted upon. (The person or thing acting upon the subject may be expressed in a prepositional phrase starting with *by*.)

A verb phrase in the passive voice is made up from a form of the verb *be* and the past participle of the main verb.

> active: The reporter *wrote* the article on Tuesday. (*The reporter* is both the subject and the performer of the action of writing.)

> passive: The article *was written* on Tuesday (by the reporter). (*The reporter* is still the performer of the action, but now *the article* is the subject.)

A. In most cases, the active voice is preferred because it is clearer and more direct. However, there are instances when the passive voice is more effective. These include (1) when the performer of the action is unknown or unimportant (or when it is so obvious that it does not need to be mentioned); (2) when you want to focus attention on the receiver, rather than the performer, of the action.

Look through the transcript and find five instances where the passive voice is used. In each case, decide who the subject of an active sentence would be. Then discuss why the passive, rather than the active, verb form is used in each case.

B. Some verbs cannot be made passive either because they do not take objects or because a passive form simply would not make sense. Note the italicized verb in each of the following sentences.

> Marilyn Burger *works* at the New York Times. (Here "work" is being used in a sense which cannot take an object.)

> The Sunday New York Times *costs* $1.50 on the newsstand. (The meaning of "cost" is such that a passive form would not make sense.)

In each of the following sentences, decide whether it is possible to make a passive sentence. If it is possible, write the passive sentence on the line provided. Include a "by phrase" if you think it makes sense to do so. If the verb cannot be made passive, simply write an [x] on that line.

1. For the sake of good taste, the Times *keeps* the names of advance obituary "clients" confidential.

_____

_____

_____

2. The great majority of people *don't like* to speak to an advance obituary writer.

_____

_____

_____

3. The writers *will take* from two days to a number of weeks to compose an obituary.

_____

_____

_____

4. The morgue *contains* many thousands of advance obituaries.

_____

_____

_____

5. The advance obituary writers *take* pride in ensuring that they *give* important figures the farewell they deserve. (Make both "take" and "give" into passive verbs.)

_____

_____

_____

After Listening

Your group is the editorial board of a major newspaper. Together, you must decide how the paper will report the deaths of four people who have passed away in the past twenty-four hours. The amount of attention you give to each person's death will be a measure of how important you consider his or her life to have been. The following types of stories are available to you:

- a long story, starting on the front page
- a medium-length story on the obituary page
- a shorter story on the obituary page
- a one-paragraph "death notice"

As a group, read the descriptions below and decide what type of article will be used to remember each person. When you have finished, explain your choices to the class.

1. Carmela Dwyer, a beautiful twenty-three-year-old model, had appeared on the cover of many magazines. She had also appeared in one movie and, though she was not a very good actress, had become very popular. She died in a car crash.

2. James Feeley was a physicist who did important work in the 1940s leading to the creation of the atomic bomb. Because of the need for secrecy, his work was never publicized, and he did not become well known. Among scientists, however, he was regarded as one of the great minds of the century. He died at age eighty-eight of natural causes.

3. Etta Morris was a single mother who lived in a low-income, high-crime housing project. Although she never finished high school, she worked two full-time jobs in order to support her family. Because of her dedication, all five of her children finished college and now have successful professional careers. Two years ago she was featured on a TV show that presented stories of "real life heroes." She died of cancer at sixty-seven.

4. Real estate developer Jimmy Zhai was one of the country's richest men. His company built shopping malls and housing developments all over the Northeastern United States. He was rumored to have connections with organized crime, but the charges were never proven. He loved to receive attention, and newspapers and TV shows often carried stories about his opulent lifestyle. He died at age fifty-four in a speedboat accident.

WRITING ACTIVITIES

Choose one of the following topics.

A. How do you want to be remembered after you are gone? Write an essay in which you describe what you would like to accomplish in life. What things have you already accomplished? Which are the major goals still before you?

B. Write an advance obituary for someone you know personally, for a famous person you admire, or for yourself. Be sure to cover the person's place of birth, job or profession, and greatest accomplishment. Beyond that, do your best, as Peter Flint says, to "capture as . . . effectively as possible the essence of a special human being."

PROJECT ACTIVITY: NEWSPAPER ARTICLE PRESENTATION

Find an article from an American newspaper that you find interesting and that you think shows something about the culture of the United States. (If the article is long, check with your teacher to see whether it can be shortened.) Read the article carefully.

When you are ready, present your article to your class in the following way. First, identify the source of the article (What newspaper does it come from? When was it published?). Then explain what kind of article it is (A news story? A feature story? An opinion piece?). Next, summarize the main points of the article for the class in your own words. You may also want to present five to ten key words necessary to understanding the article. Define them in English and explain how they are important to the story. Finally, explain what you think this article shows about U.S. culture.

"It's an uninhibited diary. It's tell all, show all. It's spontaneous. I type it as it comes and I don't correct it and I don't edit it."

Photo by Harvey Wang

7 Diaryman

Before Listening

ORIENTATION

Take five or ten minutes to write the story of your day yesterday on the lines provided below. What kind of things did you do, see, eat, etc.? Did anything particularly interesting happen—anything really worth writing about?

_____

_____

_____

_____

_____

_____

_____

_____

_____

_____

B. Share your writing with a partner, and then discuss the following:

1. How did you decide what to include and what to leave out?
2. Did you write only about events, or also about your feelings?

VOCABULARY

With a partner, read each of the following sentences. Note the italicized word. Then find the definition for the word. Write the letter next to the definition in the space provided. The first one has been done for you.

_____b_____ 1. You should never read another person's *diary* without their permission.

_____ 2. I've never heard of that book. Do you know the *author*'s name?

_____ 3. A celebrity often hires another person to help him or her write an *autobiography*.

_____ 4. While backpacking around Europe, I kept a *journal* of my thoughts and impressions.

_____ 5. To learn more about China, I read a *biography* of Mao Zedong.

_____ 6. A good *journalist* must be both persistent and open-minded.

_____ 7. Fierce Attachments, by Vivian Gornick, is a *memoir* of the author's relationship with her mother.

_____ 8. I can't meet tomorrow. What's your *schedule* like later in the week?

_____ 9. The life of a *writer* is often solitary because the work is usually done in private.

a. the person who creates a piece of writing; a writer
b. a record of events or observations (in particular, personal ones) kept daily or at frequent intervals; a journal

c. a plan or timetable for future events or appointments

d. a person who practices writing as an occupation, or one who simply writes regularly

e. the story of a person's life, as told by that person

f. a written record of a journey, or simply of life; a diary

g. a reporter or other person who writes or edits material for a newspaper, magazine, etc.

h. an account of the personal experiences of an author

i. a written history of a person's life

Listening and Understanding

INTRODUCTION

Robert Shields is a very precise man. For example, he knows that on the date this story was recorded, his diary contained exactly 34,263,395 words. Robert Shields has been keeping this diary, carefully noting everything he does, everything he says, everything he sees, everything he dreams even, for nearly three decades.

FIRST LISTENING: PREDICTING

Robert Shields says that his diary is complete. What kinds of things do you think he includes in it? Write your predictions on the following lines. Be as specific as possible.

_____

_____

_____

_____

Now listen to the broadcast. Don't worry about understanding everything about the story. You'll have a chance to hear it again. Listen to check on your predictions.

LISTENING FOR COMPREHENSION

A. As you listen to the story again, take notes on whatever you hear Robert Shields say about each of the following topics. Then answer the questions that follow by writing your responses on the lines which are provided.

His Family:	What He Eats:
The Weather:	**His Feelings:**
Prices:	**Miscellaneous:**

B. Now answer the following questions. Use your notes to help you. Write your responses on the lines provided.

1. What kind of things does Robert Shields seem to be most interested in?

_____

_____

2. What kinds of things does he leave out of his diary?

_____

_____

3. Why do you think David Isay says that Robert Shields "writes and lives" in Dayton, Washington?

_____

_____

LANGUAGE FOCUS A: UNITS OF MEASURE

Robert Shields tends to describe the world by reporting measurements in terms of numbers and units of measure, such as *ounces, pounds, dollars,* etc. For example, he describes his lunch as follows.

> I ate . . . Alaska Red salmon by Bumblebee, about seven ounces, drank ten ounces of orange juice.

In this sentence both the unit of measure and the numeral are spelled out (*seven ounces; ten ounces*). However, we often use abbreviations for such measure words—for example *oz.* rather than *ounces.* When this is done, Robert Shields's lunch would be written as follows.

> I ate . . . Alaska Red salmon by Bumblebee, about 7 oz., drank 10 oz. of orange juice.

The words are pronounced the same whether they are spelled out or abbreviated, and the abbreviations are the same for both the singular and plural forms.

A. First, read the units of measure and their abbreviations in the left-hand column. Then match the item measured in the right column to the appropriate unit of measure. Write the letter next to unit in the space provided.

Measure Word (and Abbreviation)	Item Measured
_____ 1. ounces (oz.)	a. the dimensions of a flat surface (such as a sheet of paper)
_____ 2. by (x)	b. baked goods
_____ 3. pounds (lbs.)	c. typing speed
_____ 4. words per minute (wpm)	d. the weight of relatively light objects (or volume of liquids)
_____ 5. a dozen (doz.)	e. temperature
_____ 6. dollars or cents ($ or ¢) per lb.	f. the weight of relatively heavy objects
_____ 7. degrees (°)	g. the price of food

B. Answer each of the following questions with information from the tapescript using a number and the appropriate abbreviation or symbol. Write your responses on the lines provided. You may use a dictionary for help. Read each response aloud with a partner to make sure that you are pronouncing the abbreviation correctly. The first one has been done for you.

1. What size paper is the diary typed on? __11″ x 14″__ (pronounced, "eleven inches by fourteen inches")

2. How much did the *Tri-City Herald* weigh? _____

3. How fast could Robert Shields's father type? _____

4. How many cookies did Robert Shields eat? _____

5. How much milk did he drink with his cookies? _____

6. How much has the price of bacon increased? _____

7. What is the temperature on Robert Shields's porch? _____

8. On his porch floor? _____

LISTENING FOR ANALYSIS

Listen to the broadcast again to answer the following questions. As you listen, follow along with the transcript and underline passages that provide support for your responses. Write your responses on the lines provided. You can also mark any places where the meaning of the story is unclear and ask your teacher for an explanation.

1. What unusual or surprising information does the diary contain?

_____

_____

_____

2. What unusual or surprising information do you learn about Robert Shields?

_____

_____

_____

3. Do you think Robert Shields's journal writing is truly crazy or simply eccentric? Explain.

_____

_____

_____

LANGUAGE FOCUS B: VOCABULARY IN CONTEXT (2)

Chapter 1 introduced the idea of using context clues—the words or sentences before and after a new vocabulary item—to help you figure out the meaning of a word.

In each of the two paragraphs from the story that follow, David Isay uses a number of words that you might not be familiar with. But if you look at each paragraph as a whole, you should be able to figure out the meaning of each italicized word. Write the letter of the appropriate definition in the space after each italicized word. The first one has been done for you.

David Isay describes Robert Shields:

Robert Shields is seventy-five years old. He is a short,
round man with an 1. *impish* _____c_____ grin,
decked out in his 2. *customary* _____ writing
3. *garb* _____ — navy blue thermal underwear
and a white T-shirt. Shields was a minister and high-
school English teacher in this 4. *picturesque* _____
Washington town before 5. *devoting* _____
himself to his journal.

David Isay gives his personal reaction to Robert Shields's obsession with
his diary:

It is somewhat 6. *disconcerting* _____ to see the
extent to which this task has taken over the life of
Reverend Robert Shields, chaining him to his typewriter
on this endless 7. *endeavor* _____. Shields,
it seems, is so busy documenting the 8. *insignificant*
_____ 9. *minutiae* _____ of his life that
he has become 10. *oblivious to* _____ everything
else going on around him.

a. upsetting; bothersome
b. pretty; lovely
c. mischievous
d. small details
e. unimportant
f. usual; habitual
g. completely unaware of
h. a job or task that requires effort
i. clothing
j. dedicating; committing

After Listening

DISCUSSION ACTIVITIES

With your group, choose one of the following activities.

A. Do you think you would enjoy knowing Robert Shields? Why or why not? Support your answer by referring to specific things he does or says in the broadcast.

B. How important a role does writing play in your day-to-day life? What kinds of things do you write? How would your life be different if you tried to get by without writing anything?

WRITING ACTIVITIES

Choose one of the following activities

A. Reread what you wrote for the Orientation. Choose one sentence that you find interesting. Write about the idea in that sentence or whatever idea that sentence leads you to. Try not to be like Robert Shields, who mentions everything without going into depth about anything. Instead, try to describe the experience as fully as you can so that your readers will really understand what the experience was like for you.

B. Between now and the next meeting of the class, become a "diaryperson" by keeping your own minute-by-minute diary of everything you do. Keep it up for as long as you can. You can write it in the same style as Robert Shields or in another style that you prefer, but do not leave any gaps.

Bring to class a sample of the diary (covering perhaps an hour or two) and share it with the class. Tell them how it felt to have to write down everything. Did keeping this diary affect the things you chose to do? Did it change the way you feel about Robert Shields and his diary? What other reactions did you have?

PROJECT ACTIVITY: SURVEY ON WRITING

Your teacher will assign you one of the following questions. Make sure that you understand the question, and then take a poll of your classmates' responses. Use a chart, such as the one below. Ask each classmate the question and take notes on his or her response. When you have polled everybody, report the results to your class.

1. Do you enjoy writing?

2. Who is your favorite author? What do you like about this writer's work?

3. What's the longest book you've ever read? How long did it take you to read it?

4. Have you ever kept a diary? What kinds of things did you write about?

5. Have you ever read anyone's published diaries? Whose?

6. Should parents ever read their children's diaries without their permission? Why or why not?

7. Have you ever read *Anne Frank: The Diary of a Young Girl*? What do you know about her?

8. What would you do if someone read your diary without your permission?

9. Which do you spend more time reading: newspapers, magazines, or books?

10. How fast can you type?

Do You Enjoy Writing?

Classmate	Response
1. Keiko	likes poetry sometimes, but not writing essays for school
2. Rodrigo	really likes writing, wants to be a journalist after finishing school
3.	

"The sickly sweet grape juice taste of Passover wine, so thick it coats the mouth, always takes me back to my childhood Seders."

Photo by Harvey Wang

8 Passover Wine

Before Listening

ORIENTATION

First, read the following definitions for *Passover* and *Seder*.

Passover ('pas-ō-vər) *n.*, *Judaism.* A Jewish holiday celebrated for eight days on the seventh month of the year in the Jewish calendar. Passover commemorates the liberation of the ancient Hebrews from slavery in Egypt.

Seder ('sā-dər) *n.*, *Judaism.* The feast commemorating the exodus of the Jews from Egypt, celebrated on the first two nights of Passover. At a Seder, exodus is remembered by eating foods of symbolic significance, reciting prayers and stories, and drinking sacramental wine.

Now, think of a holiday that your family celebrates. Write a dictionary definition of the holiday on the lines provided. Think about how you would describe this holiday to someone who had never heard about it before.

_____

_____

_____

_____

Share what you wrote with your group. In addition to your dictionary definition, tell your group what this holiday means to you personally.

VOCABULARY

The words below refer to wine and winemaking. First, read each of the words. Then find the definition for each word. Write the letter next to the definition in the space provided. The first one has been done for you.

_____i_____ 1. winery

_____ 2. jug

_____ 3. bottle

_____ 4. chateau

_____ 5. vat

_____ 6. vintage

_____ 7. fermentation

_____ 8. cellar

_____ 9. vineyard

_____ 10. keg

a. the most common container for wine, usually holding 750 milliliters
b. a cool, underground place where wine can be stored
c. a small barrel, usually holding less than ten gallons
d. a large open container where grapes are crushed
e. a container for liquids bigger than a bottle, with a handle

f. a French word which can refer to a winery or to a large country house and estate

g. the year in which a particular wine was made

h. the process by which the juice of grapes is turned into wine

i. the entire establishment where wine is made

j. land where grapevines are grown

Dictionary Note

Although *wine* and *vineyard* start with different letters, they both come from the same Latin root, *vinum*, which means "wine." What other words related to wine come from this root? Check your ideas in a dictionary.

Listening and Understanding

INTRODUCTION

Even since his youth, David Isay has been celebrating Passover Seders and drinking the special wine that is served there. Passover wine is a sweet, thick wine that has been blessed by rabbis. In this broadcast, David visits America's oldest family-owned kosher winery, where he gets to know the owners and some of the customers.

FIRST LISTENING: PREDICTING

Write your responses to the questions below on the lines provided.

1. What kinds of personal connections do you think that David Isay will have with Passover wine?

_____

_____

2. What do you think the atmosphere of a family-owned winery would be like? Explain.

_____

_____

Listen to the broadcast to check on the answers to your predictions. Don't worry about understanding everything in the story. You'll have a chance to hear it again.

LISTENING FOR COMPREHENSION

Read over the following questions and see whether there are any that you can answer from your first listening. Then listen to the broadcast again to check your answers and to find the answers to the remaining questions.

1. What kind of building is Schapiro's Wine in? What is the store like inside?

_____

_____

2. How long has Schapiro's been open? Have they ever had to stop selling wine? Explain.

_____

_____

_____

3. Where was Schapiro's wine made in the past? Where is it made today?

_____

_____

4. Why do customers remain loyal to Schapiro's?

_____

_____

5. What is Linda Schapiro like?

_____

6. What is the most popular spot at Schapiro's?

_____

7. What associations does David Isay have with Passover wine?

_____

_____

8. Is Schapiro's Wines in danger of going out of business? Explain.

_____

_____

LANGUAGE FOCUS A: USING "WOULD" AND "USED TO"

In the broadcast, many of the characters talk about their memories associated with Passover wine. In doing so, they sometimes use the forms *would* and *used to* in order to express an action that was regularly repeated in the past. For example, note the use of *would* and *used to* in the following sentences.

> When I was a little girl, my father *used to* buy a gallon and we'd have it for the whole year.

> When I was a little girl, my father *would* buy a gallon and we'd have it for the whole year.

Note that *used to* can also be used to express a past situation that no longer exists. *Would* can not be used in this way. *Would* is only used for past actions that were repeated, not those that simply continued. For example, note the use of *used to* and *would* in the following sentence.

> Correct: There *used to* be a store around here selling Jewish horseradish.

> Incorrect: There *would* be a store around here selling Jewish horseradish.

A. In each of the sentences below, determine whether you can use either *used to* and *would* before the verb in parentheses or only *used to* is acceptable. If either form can be used, write the correct form of each on the line provided. If only *used to* is acceptable, write it on the line. The first two have been done for you.

1. I _used to live_ (*live*) in Barcelona, in the old quarter.

2. In the mornings, I _used to do/would do_ (*do*) all my shopping in the local market.

3. In those days, I _____ (*speak*) Catalan fluently. Now, I don't speak it as well.

4. I _____ (*bargain*) with the shopkeepers to get a good price.

5. There also _____ (*be*) a newspaper vendor I enjoyed talking to.

6. In the evenings, I _____ (*eat*) in a lot of the local restaurants.

7. In the restaurants, I often _____ (*see*) my neighbors.

8. We _____ (*talk*) about things going on in the neighborhood.

9. After dinner, I _____ (*help*) some of the local kids with their English homework.

B. Write a paragraph in which you reminisce about some part of your childhood. For example, you might choose to write about how your family spent your summer holidays. Use the forms *used to* and *would* according the rules presented above.

LISTENING FOR ANALYSIS

One thing that makes Schapiro's Wines special is the way Linda and Norman interact with their customers. For example, note how Linda describes the store.

> It's very informal, you see, this is not IBM. The office is always open, it's Linda and Norman. . . . You can fight with me, you can argue, you can use the telephone. . . . It's just not, you know, *hoi polloi*.

Listen to the broadcast again for answers to the following questions. As you listen, follow along with the transcript and underline passages that provide support for your responses. Write your responses on the lines provided. You can also mark any places where the meaning of the story is unclear and ask your teacher for an explanation.

1. What parts of the broadcast show that the atmosphere in Schapiro's is informal?

_____

_____

2. Are there any points when the atmosphere is not informal? When?

_____

_____

3. Do you think you would enjoy shopping at a store like Schapiro's? Why or why not?

_____

_____

LANGUAGE FOCUS B: USING THE PASSIVE VOICE TO DESCRIBE A PROCESS

Read the following passage that describes the process of making wine. Note that the italicized verbs are in the passive voice.

> Today the grapes *are crushed* at vineyards in upstate
> New York, but they *are trucked* here to ferment in
> Schapiro's cavernous cellar.

The verbs are in the passive voice because the focus is on the thing receiving the action—the grapes—rather than on the person or people performing the action. (For a review of the passive voice, refer to Language Focus B in Chapter 6.)

A. The paragraph below describes the process for making applesauce. First, read the verbs in the box. Then read the paragraph. Choose the correct verb from the box to complete each item. Write the correct form of the verb in the space provided. Most of the verbs will be in the passive voice. The first two have been done for you.

core	pick
ship	move
pack (used twice)	cook
transport	remain
change	peel
blend	load (used twice)
label	

First, the apples 1. _are picked_ in the orchard and 2. _(are) packed_ into large crates. The crates 3. _____ onto trucks that 4. _____ the apples to the applesauce factory. At the factory, the apples 5. _____ and 6. _____. When only the flesh of the apple 7. _____, it 8. _____ down and 9. _____ until smooth. This process 10. _____ the apples into applesauce. Next, the applesauce 11. _____ into bottles that 12. _____ along an assembly line where they 13. _____. Then the bottles 14. _____ onto trucks and 15. _____ out to stores.

B. Think of another process that takes place in a number of steps. Write a paragraph describing the process, keeping the focus on the thing that is undergoing the process (like the wine and the apples in the descriptions above). In writing your paragraph, use the passive voice wherever it is appropriate.

After Listening

DISCUSSION ACTIVITY

Think about something memorable that happened during a family gathering when you were a child. It could be something funny, sad, exciting, etc. First, take five to ten minutes to jot down everything you can remember about what happened and how you felt. Then tell your group the story of what happened in as much detail as you can.

WRITING ACTIVITIES

Choose one of the following topics.

A. Write about a tradition that was an important part of your family life while you were growing up. Explain what it meant to your family and to you as an individual. Do you think it is important that this tradition be passed on to your children? Explain why or why not. (If you choose to write about a tradition connected to the event that you discussed in the Discussion Activity, you can use the notes that you made then as a starting point.)

B. In many places in the United States today, large chain stores are opening up and competing with small "mom and pop" stores like Schapiro's Wines. What kinds of stores do you prefer to shop at—small, personal ones, or larger, more impersonal ones? Write an essay in which you explain your preference. Be sure to give examples that show what you like about the type of store you prefer.

PROJECT ACTIVITY: RESEARCHING AN ETHNIC HOLIDAY

As a nation of immigrants, the United States has many different ethnic groups, each of which celebrates its own holidays. Research a holiday that is celebrated by an ethnic group other than your own in the United States. You may choose from the list below, or you may come up with another group.

Ethnic Group	Holiday
African-American	Kwanza
Chinese	Spring Festival (Lunar New Year's Day)
German	Oktoberfest
Irish	St. Patrick's Day
Islamic (Muslim)	Ramadan
Japanese	O-shougatsu (New Year's Holiday)
Jewish	Passover
Mexican	Cinco de Mayo
Russian	Orthodox Christmas

Find out when the holiday is celebrated, what it commemorates, and how it is observed (for example, what kind of food is eaten, what ceremonies are held, etc.). You can get this information from an encyclopedia or other reference book, by searching on the internet, or by speaking to a member of that ethnic group. When you have gathered the information, report your findings to your class.

Photo by Harvey Wang

"I've had dancing dentists,
singing lawyers, cab drivers
who do handwriting analysis.
You name it, I've had it.
And if I haven't had it,
I'll create it."

9 The Joe Franklin Show

Before Listening

ORIENTATION

What is your favorite television show? Tell your group about a TV show you like to watch. Explain where the show takes place, who the main characters are, and anything else your group should know about it. Also, tell your group why you like the show.

VOCABULARY

A. First, read the categories of TV shows listed below. Then, with your group, describe each category and give at least two examples shows that belong to it.

1. cartoon
2. soap opera
3. talk show
4. news program

5. "sitcom" (situation comedy)
6. drama
7. miniseries

B. Answer each of the following questions. Write your responses on the lines provided. Discuss your responses with your group.

1. Which category best describes the show you talked about in the Orientation?

_____

2. Which kind of shows are most popular in your home country?

_____

_____

3. What other kinds of shows can you think of, besides those listed?

_____

_____

Listening and Understanding

INTRODUCTION

It is difficult to give an introduction to Joe Franklin because *he* is famous for giving introductions as a TV talk show host. As a matter of fact, Joe claims to have invented the TV talk show in 1951, and he hasn't slowed down since. David Isay had a chance to visit with Joe and get a backstage look at how his show is produced.

FIRST LISTENING: PREDICTING

Look at the photo of Joe Franklin in his office on page 81. What do you think his personality might be like? Write your response on the lines provided.

_____

_____

_____

_____

Listen to the broadcast to check on the answers to your predictions. Don't worry about understanding everything in the story. You'll have a chance to hear it again.

Listening for Comprehension

Read over the following questions and see whether there are any you can answer from your first listening. Then listen to the broadcast again to check your answers and to find the answers to the remaining questions.

1. For each of the following questions, circle the correct response. According to Joe . . .

   a. How many phone calls does he get each day?   10   100   1,000

   b. How many years has his talk show been on the air?   4   14   40

   c. How many episodes has he hosted?   280   2,800   28,000

   d. How many guests has he interviewed?   25,000   250,000   2.5 million

2. Did the TV station Joe worked for forty years ago think that his plan for a TV talk show was a good idea? Explain.

   _____

   _____

3. What does Joe do before he has to go on the air? Does he seem nervous?

   _____

   _____

4. What kind of introduction does Joe give his guests?

   _____

   _____

5. According to Joe, how has he managed to stay on the air so long?

   _____

6. Does Joe allow his guests to promote themselves or their products? If yes, give an example.

_____

_____

_____

7. When does Joe plan to give up the show and retire?

_____

8. What kind of mood is Joe in at the end of his long day?

_____

_____

LANGUAGE FOCUS A: GROUPS OF SYNONYMS

One distinctive feature of Joe Franklin's speaking style is his use of multiple synonyms (words that mean the same thing) one right after the other. Note the italicized synonyms in the following sentence.

> How about if I do a show of people talking *nose to nose, eyeball to eyeball, face to face, toe to toe?*

A. Read over each of the sentences below and note the italicized word or phrase. Then find the synonym or group of synonyms for each one. Write the letter next to the synonym in the space provided.

_____1. Dan, I need you *maniacally*, _____.

_____2. Tell them things are *concretizing*, things are _____, they're _____.

_____3. We've got one of the *most famed* of all the plastic surgeons, a man who's _____ . . .

_____4. The excitement is *mounting*, the excitement is _____ because everybody says, "Joe, is she really here, the rock and roll madam?"

_____5. I'm the last one who's *organic* or _____.

I'm _____.

_____6. I would say that today's shows were superb. That's *my informed appraisal,* _____.

a. coming together . . . coagulating
b. my educated assessment, my considered opinion
c. mushrooming and skyrocketing and snowballing and escalating
d. pathologically
e. from the bones . . . not plastic
f. all over the headlines

B. Discuss the following questions with your group. What effect does Joe's use of groups of synonyms have on the listener? How does this aspect of his speaking style relate to what you said about Joe's personality in the First Listening: Predicting exercise?

LISTENING FOR ANALYSIS

Listen to the broadcast for answers to the following questions. As you listen, follow along with the transcript and underline passages that provide support for your responses. Write your responses on the lines provided. You can also mark any places in the transcript where the meaning of the story is unclear and ask your teacher for an explanation.

1. At which points in the story do you think Joe is stretching the truth? What makes you think that? (Consider both what Joe says and also his tone of voice.)

_____

_____

_____

_____

2. What indications does David Isay give that he doesn't always believe what Joe is saying?

_____

_____

_____

LANGUAGE FOCUS B: THE LANGUAGE OF HYPE

Another distinctive feature of Joe Franklin's speaking style is that he often uses "hype"—colorful language that makes exaggerated claims in order to impress the listener. (Joe's use of hype may be one reason we tend to doubt that he is always telling the truth.)

Note the use of hype in the following sentence from the broadcast.

> Richard, I want to tell you something. I've got so many surprises for you. Let's talk tonight at seven o'clock, you promise? It's critical.

A. For each section listed below, look through the transcript to find three examples of hype.

1. During Joe's phone conversations:

   a. _____

   b. _____

   c. _____

2. In Joe's introductions of his guests:

   a. _____

   b. _____

   c. _____

B. Sometimes David Isay uses exaggerated language to describe Joe and his show. Look through the transcript to find the exaggerated word or phrase that means the same as each of the following phrases. (The lines in the transcript are given.)

1. very, very messy (lines 1–5) _____

2. always fun to watch (lines 135–140) _____

C. Imagine that each member of your group is going to appear as a guest on "The Joe Franklin Show." Write a hyped-up introduction—the type that Joe Franklin would give. Start with something that is true about each person. Then create the introduction, using hype, or exaggerated claims similar to the ones Joe makes. (For example, a student who enjoys bicycling could be introduced as "one of the top recreational cyclists in the world.") Present your introductions to your class.

After Listening

DISCUSSION ACTIVITIES

With your group, choose one of the following activities.

A. Tell your group how much time you spend watching television in an average week. What kinds of programs do you usually watch? Overall, do you think watching TV has a positive or negative effect on your life? Explain.

B. What is the effect of American television programs on other cultures? Explain to your group how much of the TV programming in your home country comes from the United States and what kinds of shows they are. How do these shows affect the view of the United States in your home country? How does watching American television affect the culture of your country?

WRITING ACTIVITIES

Choose one of the following topics:

A. Suppose that television were suddenly eliminated. Write an essay in which you describe the effects this change would have. You may concentrate on how the elimination of TV would affect your own life, or on how it would affect society in general.

B. Do you think celebrities are good role models for children? Write an essay in which you express your opinion and support it by giving reasons and examples.

PROJECT ACTIVITY: PRODUCING A TV TALK SHOW

Your group is going to put on its own TV talk show. Determine who will be the host and who will play the guests. Plan what you will do during the show. Who will the guests be? Why will they be appearing on the show? (A guest usually wants to promote a book, a movie, or another product.) How will the host introduce each guest? What questions will he or she ask each one?

The show should begin with an opening monologue in which the host tells a couple of jokes or stories and then announces who will be on the show. After the monologue, the host should interview the first guest.

When you are ready, your group will perform its show for the rest of the class. If possible, your teacher can videotape your presentation so that you can watch it as you would a real TV talk show.

"I woke up one morning in a cold sweat. 'What am I going to do with those wedding rings?' So God spoke to me and said, 'Maybe a wedding chapel would be a good thing to put in that pawnshop.'"

Photo by Harvey Wang

10
Kipperman's Pawnshop and Wedding Chapel

Before Listening

ORIENTATION

How many words do you know that have to do with weddings? Divide a sheet of paper into three columns. Label the first column "People," the second column "Events," and the third column "Things." First, for each category, brainstorm a list of words that are associated with getting married. Then explain how each word fits into the process of getting married.

People	Events	Things

VOCABULARY

A. With a partner, read each of the following words or phrases. Then find the definition for each one below. Write the letter next to the definition in the space provided. You may use a dictionary, if you wish. The first one has been done for you.

_____F_____ 1. a pawnshop

_____ 2. wedding chapel

_____ 3. to be ordained

_____ 4. to hock

_____ 5. newlyweds

_____ 6. an annulment

_____ 7. a penitentiary

_____ 8. divine inspiration

_____ 9. a divorce

_____10. stained-glass windows

a. a slang word meaning to get a loan from a pawnshop

b. a creative influence from God or a god

c. recently married people

d. windows with designs made of colored glass, often found in a church

e. a declaration that a marriage is invalid

f. a business in which valuable objects are traded in as security for short-term loans

g. a legal and formal dissolution of a marriage

h. a prison for persons convicted of serious crimes

i. a small churchlike room where marriage ceremonies are performed

j. to become a religious officer such as a minister, priest, or rabbi

B. With your partner, discuss the associations you have for each word or phrase. Which of the words relate to religious or spiritual ideas? Which relate to more earthly or nonspiritual ideas? Check your ideas with your teacher.

Listening and Understanding

INTRODUCTION

There are a lot of pawnshops in the United States. But as far as we know, Ted Kipperman's place is the only combination pawnshop/wedding chapel. This business has some advantages. For example, if you buy a wedding ring at Kipperman's pawnshop, he will give you a free wedding in his chapel. David Isay visited Kipperman's and even got to participate in a very unusual wedding that took place there.

FIRST LISTENING: PREDICTING

How would you expect a wedding held in a pawnshop be different from a traditional wedding? On the lines provided, write down all the differences that you would expect to find.

_____

_____

_____

_____

_____

Listen to the broadcast to check on the answers to your predictions. Don't worry about understanding everything in the story. You'll have a chance to hear it again.

LISTENING FOR COMPREHENSION

Read over the following questions and see whether there are any you can answer from your first listening. Then listen to the broadcast again to check your answers and to find the answers to the remaining questions.

1. Why does Ted Kipperman's business stand out in the neighborhood where it's located?

_____

2. What things typical of a pawnshop are sold at Kipperman's? List as many as you can.

_____

_____

3. What led Ted Kipperman to start offering weddings at his pawnshop?

_____

_____

4. Why did Ernest and Lucy decide to have their wedding at Kipperman's?

_____

_____

5. Which "extras" do the Durans decide to have in their wedding?

_____

_____

6. Does Ted Kipperman perform annulments? Why or why not?

_____

_____

7. What is unusual about Rose and Michael's wedding?

_____

8. How does David Isay help the couple to get married?

_____

LANGUAGE FOCUS A: PHRASAL VERBS (2)

Phrasal verbs, which were introduced in Chapter 1, consist of a verb and one or more prepositions that combine to express an idiomatic meaning (a meaning that can't be predicted from knowing the meaning of each word alone). Phrasal verbs can be difficult to learn because their meanings are not always predictable and can change greatly with context.

For example, in the following sentence from the broadcast, the phrasal verb *take up* means "to occupy or use up space."

> An enormous painted portrait of Ted Kipperman
> *takes up* an entire side of the building.

But in another context, *take up* can also mean "to begin a new activity," as in the following sentence.

> I have a lot of free time these days, so I've decided to
> *take up* golf.

Each of the following phrasal verbs from the broadcast is followed by definitions of some of the different meanings it can have. Sometimes, a noun form is also given. Read over each of definitions. Then, in the lettered examples, match the italicized multiword verb (or its noun form) with the appropriate definition. The first one has been done for you as an example.

1. **stand out** 1. To be noticeably different in some way.
   2. (n.) One who is exceptionally good at something.

_____1_____ a. Because it is so colorful, Kipperman's Pawnshop *stands out* from the grungy strip of fast-food joints, beauty parlors, and liquor stores that surround it.

_____2_____ b. In his youth, he was a real *standout* on the soccer field, but now he's in terrible shape.

2. **come in** 1. To enter. 2. To arrive at a scheduled location. 3. To be relevant.

_____ a. Once in a while, people *come in* and tell Ted Kipperman that they don't want their wedding rings anymore.

_____ b. I don't see where money *comes in* to our discussion. We were talking about what's the right thing to do.

_____ c. My plane was supposed to *come in* at 7:30, but it was almost two hours late.

3. **pass on** 1. Give to another person, often of a following generation. 2. Decide not to buy or take; refuse an offer.

_____ a. Ernest and Lucy have opted for Kipperman's bargain basement wedding, *passing on* all of the extras he offers.

_____ b. I have put a good deal of care into assembling my collection, and I hope to *pass* it *on* to my children some day.

4. **come out** 1. To exit or be released from some place. 2. To become widely known, as information. 3. To become available for sale.

_____ a. By the time he *comes out* of jail, Michael Smith and his wife will both be fifty-some years old.

_____ b. I'm ready to buy a new car, but I think I'll wait until the new models *come out* in the fall.

_____ c. By the time the truth *came out* about the false charges, it was too late. The politician's reputation had already be ruined.

5. **pick up** 1. To lift, as with one's hand. 2. To collect something from a store. 3. To give someone a ride. 4. To make neater; to tidy. 5. To meet and become (sexually) involved with a person. 6. (n.) A small truck with an open back.

_____ a. Ted Kipperman says that most people *pick up* their wedding rings after they pawn them.

_____ b. After his divorce, my brother started going to bars in order to *pick up* women.

_____ c. I know that a car would be more comfortable, but I enjoy driving my *pickup*.

_____ d. I can *pick* you *up* on my way downtown and give you a ride to the party.

_____ e. The box was too heavy for me to *pick up*, so I had to drag it to the place I wanted it.

_____ f. I was feeling somewhat down, but *picking up* my living room put me into a better state of mind.

Listening for Analysis

Listen to the broadcast again for answers to the following questions. As you listen, follow along with the transcript and underline passages that provide support for your responses. Write your responses on the lines provided. You can also mark any places where the meaning of the story is unclear and ask your teacher for an explanation.

Many people would agree that much of Ted Kipperman's business—including the idea of holding weddings in a pawnshop—is in poor taste.

1. In your opinion, what parts of the story show that Kipperman has bad taste?

_____

_____

_____

2. Do you think it would be fun to visit a place like Kipperman's? Why or why not?

_____

_____

3. Would you ever want to get married at a place like Kipperman's? Why or why not?

_____

_____

LANGUAGE FOCUS B: FORMULAIC LANGUAGE

Much of the language used in performing wedding ceremonies is highly formulaic. That is, it uses words and phrases particular to the situation and uncommon in everyday English.

Note the sentence that Ted Kipperman uses to begin the wedding ceremony for Michael and Rosario.

> Dearly beloved, we are gathered here today to join
> Michael and Rosario in marriage.

This formula reminds everyone of the purpose of the gathering and identifies the people who are getting married. The phrases "dearly beloved" and "we are gathered here today" are usually used at weddings and are not often used in everyday English. In everyday English, this meaning might be expressed in the following way.

> The reason we are all here today is to celebrate the
> wedding between Michael and Rosario.

A. Read each of the following examples of formulaic language taken from the broadcast. Then, on the lines provided, answer the questions that follow.

> 1. Rosario, do you take Michael to be your lawful
> wedded husband? To live with him according to God's
> holy ordinances?

a. What function does this formula perform? _____

b. How would you express this idea in everyday English? _____

_____

2. By the authority of the state of Texas and by my authority as a chaplain, I now pronounce you husband and wife.

a. What function does this formula perform? _____

b. How would you express this idea in everyday English? _____

_____

3. Whom God has joined together let no man put asunder.

a. At what point in the ceremony does this formula occur? _____

b. How would you express this idea in everyday English? _____

_____

B. In the transcript, find three examples of formulaic language that deal with selling products and write them on the lines provided below. Then explain the purpose of each expression and the effect it is intended to have.

1. _____

_____

2. _____

_____

3. _____

_____

After Listening

DISCUSSION ACTIVITIES

With your group, choose one of the following activities.

A. Describe to your group what the perfect wedding would be like—either for yourself or your children. In your description, consider the following questions. Where would the ceremony be held? (In a church or other house of worship? Outdoors in a park? In a family home?) What kind of reception would you have afterward? (Intimate, with only family and a few close friends? Huge, with lots of guests?)

B. Do you think that the United States is too commercialized? With your group, compare the level of commercialism in the United States to that in your home countries. You may use the example of Ted Kipperman, or you may bring into the discussion any other things you have seen, read, or experienced about the United States.

WRITING ACTIVITIES

Choose one of the following topics.

A. Write an essay describing a traditional wedding in your home country. What are the special customs or traditions? How are weddings similar to or different from those in the United States? Make your description detailed enough that a reader who has never visited your country can get an idea of what it would be like to go to a wedding there.

B. A popular proverb states, "It is no use arguing about taste." This means that good or bad taste is simply a matter of opinion and cannot be discussed or explained. Do you agree with this statement, or do you think that there are some things that are clearly in bad taste? Explain your position and give at least one example which illustrates it.

PROJECT ACTIVITY: PLANNING A "COMBINATION BUSINESS"

Ted Kipperman has combined two seemingly unrelated ideas—a pawnshop and a wedding chapel—into a single business. With your group, make a plan for your own "combination business." Consider each of the following questions.

1. How will the two elements of your business complement each other? (At Kipperman's Pawnshop, the wedding rings that are pawned can then be sold to people who want to get married in the chapel.)

2. What kind of advertising will you do? (Will you have your portraits painted on the side of the building, as Ted Kipperman has?)

3. What will the motto or slogan for your business be? (Can you come up with a better one than, "When you're in the mood to say 'I do' and you really care, think of Kipperman's Wedding Chapel, where love is always in the air"?)

When you are ready, each group will present the plan for its business to the class.

"Everybody passed by them and just told them they couldn't serve them. That made me kind of nervous, so I went on back to the back and I stayed back there."

Photo by Harvey Wang

11 Woolworth's Lunch Counter

Before Listening

ORIENTATION

With your group, discuss and write down your answers to the following questions.

1. Write down whatever you know about the Civil Rights Movement.

   a. When did it take place? _____

   b. Who were its leaders? _____

   _____

   c. What were its goals? _____

   _____

2. What role do you think ordinary people must have played in the Civil Rights Movement? _____

_____

_____

_____

VOCABULARY

With a partner, look over each of the following words relating to the Civil Rights Movement. Then write the letter for each word in the appropriate place in the paragraph below. You may use your dictionary. The first one has been done for you.

a. rights
b. prohibited
c. the 1950s
d. segregation
e. integrate
f. demonstrators
g. African-American
h. nonviolent
i. sit-in

The Civil Rights Movement, which began in 1. _c. the 1950s_, was an important period of social change in the United States. At this time, 2. _____ people did not enjoy many of the basic 3. _____ of citizenship, such as voting and equal protection under the law. Additionally, formal policies of 4. _____ throughout the southern states meant that blacks were 5. _____ from attending the same schools or using the same public facilities as whites. The Civil Rights Movement sought to address these inequalities by means of 6. _____ protest. One type of protest was the 7. _____, in which groups of 8. _____ would physically occupy a location that they wanted to 9. _____ and remain there until their demands were met.

Listening and Understanding

INTRODUCTION

Sometimes a store is more than just a store. The Woolworth's drugstore in Greensboro, North Carolina, is also a part of history. In 1960, when the Woolworth's lunch counter served food to whites only, four black men sat down there, tried to order, and sparked the beginnings of the civil rights sit-in movement. When David Isay found out that the Greensboro Woolworth's was closing down, he visited this historic lunch counter and spent some time with Geneva Tisdale, who has worked there for forty-two years.

FIRST LISTENING: PREDICTING

Before you listen to the broadcast, write three questions you would like to have answered by the story. You can write questions about Geneva Tisdale's life, the Civil Rights Movement, or anything else you would like to learn about.

1. _____

_____

2. _____

_____

3. _____

_____

Listen to the broadcast to see whether your questions are answered. Don't worry about understanding everything in the story. You'll have a chance to hear it again.

LISTENING FOR COMPREHENSION

Read over the following questions and see whether there are any you can answer from your first listening. Then listen to the broadcast again to check your answers and to find the answers to the remaining questions.

1. How long has Geneva Tisdale worked at the lunch counter? _____

_____

2. Until 1960, what restrictions were there on the jobs blacks could do at Woolworth's?

_____

_____

3. How did Geneva react when the first protesters tried to order?

_____

_____

4. How long did the first sit-in last? Was it successful? _____

_____

5. Whose idea was it for Geneva to be the first African-American to eat at the counter?

_____

6. What did she eat? _____

7. How much does Geneva earn at her job? _____

8. What hope of Geneva's will not be fulfilled? _____

_____

LANGUAGE FOCUS A: TIME PREPOSITIONS

One common use of prepositions is to express an idea relating to time. "In," "at," and "on" are the most basic prepositions used to express time ideas. "In" usually refers to a general *period of time*

> I'll see you sometime . . . in the morning, in the next week, in July, in the summer.

"At" usually refers to a more specific *point in time*.

> I'll see you . . . at 11:00 a.m. tomorrow, at the end of the month.

"On" usually refers to a given *day*.

> I'll see you . . . on Saturday, on December 20th, on your birthday.

Other time prepositions, such as "since," "for," and "until," work with verbs to describe the relation of certain actions to other actions. "For" and "since" both describe the *duration* of an activity. For is followed by *a length of time*, and since is followed by *a point in time*.

> I've lived in San Francisco . . . *since 1990, since I was twenty-five.*

> I've lived in San Francisco . . . *for nine years, for almost a decade.*

"Until" means "going up to and ending at a given point in time or event."

> *Until 1990,* I had lived in a small town my entire life.

> I lived in a small town *until I moved to San Francisco.*

Note the italicized time expression in each of the sentences below. Then write the appropriate time preposition in the blank space. The first one has been done for you.

1. At the time the Woolworth's lunch counter closed, Geneva Tisdale had worked there _____*for*_____ *more than four decades.*

2. Geneva Tisdale was around _____ *the days when African-Americans were not allowed to serve food.*

3. The policy of segregation went unchallenged _____ *February 1, 1960,* when four college students sat down at the counter as a protest.

4. "_____ *first,* I thought the protesters were just being funny."

5. _____ *the time,* Geneva Tisdale was pregnant with her third child and was sent home to wait out the sit-ins.

6. _____ *the second day* there were twenty-eight students sitting at the counter. On the third there were sixty, occupying all of the luncheonette seats all day.

7. Woolworth's and the students negotiated _____ *five months.*

8. _____ *July,* the store finally announced that there would soon be a change in policy.

9. _____ *July 25th, 1960,* Geneva Tisdale was told to come to work in her uniform but to bring along a change of clothes.

10. It was _____ *lunchtime* on that day that Geneva and her coworkers became the first African-Americans to eat at the lunch counter.

11. Geneva Tisdale says that she has not had a meal at this Woolworth's counter _____ *then.*

12. Her low salary, Geneva Tisdale says, speaks to what has not changed _____ *four young men occupied this historic lunch counter.*

13. _____ *Monday,* Geneva Tisdale will be moved out onto the floor of the store.

14. She will work there _____ *the store closes in early January.*

LISTENING FOR ANALYSIS

Listen to the broadcast again to answer the following questions. As you listen, follow along with the transcript and underline passages that provide support for your responses. You can also mark any places where the meaning of the story is unclear and ask your teacher for an explanation.

1. Geneva Tisdale has very complicated feelings about her job. What parts of the broadcast demonstrate each of the following feelings? Write your response on the lines provided.

   a. That she takes pride in her work. _____

   _____

   b. That she has some fond memories of her job. _____

   _____

c. That she feels disappointed and perhaps angry? _____

_____

2. Do you think she has a right to feel disappointed or angry? Explain your opinion by referring to the broadcast.

_____

_____

LANGUAGE FOCUS B: NONSTANDARD ENGLISH

Standard English is the most widely used variety of English. It is the English most often used in school, in business, and in the media. Nonstandard English refers to varieties of usage that are limited to a particular region, socioeconomic group, or other cultural context.

Geneva Tisdale speaks a nonstandard variety of English that is spoken by many black people in the South and throughout the United States This nonstandard English, which is sometimes called Black English or Ebonics, follows different grammatical rules than does standard English.

For example, in nonstandard English, the verb "be" can be omitted from statements about things that are generally true (this pattern is similar to that in such languages as Chinese and Russian). Note the following example.

He tall. (nonstandard English)

He is tall. (standard English)

A. Read each of the following statements taken from the broadcast. The part of the statement that reflects nonstandard English is in italics. Rewrite each, using standard English.

1. "If the sandwich-board girl quit, then she put me on the sandwich board, so *I been around.*"

_____

2. "*Have you* a big bag and all." _____

3. "Walk around like *you shopping.*" _____

4. "So *we done* that." (After Geneva's boss tells her to change back into her work clothes)

_____

5. "Now, if you don't want your pictures in the paper, order something that you can eat *real quick*."

_____

6. "It wasn't long before (a.) *the photographer and all* (b.) *was* in."

   a. _____

   b. _____

B. Discuss each of the following questions with your group.

1. How do you think the fact that Geneva Tisdale speaks a nonstandard variety of English might affect her prospects if she tried to find another job?

2. The question of whether the variety of nonstandard English that Geneva Tisdale speaks is a dialect or a separate language is a controversial one in the United States today. There is a saying about the difference between a language and a dialect that a language is "a dialect with an army." What does this saying mean? Do you agree with the idea it expresses?

After Listening

DISCUSSION ACTIVITY

Discuss each of the following questions with your group. After everyone in the group has had a chance to express his or her opinion, choose one person to summarize the group's discussion on each topic to the class.

1. Do you think Geneva Tisdale has been treated fairly by her employer? Explain your opinion.

2. Has this story given you a better understanding of the experiences of African-Americans in the United States? What have you learned? What questions do you still have?

3. Do you think that it is important to live in a racially integrated society? What role, if any, should government play in making it so?

4. Is there racial and ethnic equality in your first country today? Is there equal opportunity for all groups in terms of economic advancement, legal protection, and social integration? Compare your first country to what you know about the United States.

WRITING ACTIVITIES

Choose one of the following topics.

A. Toward the end of the broadcast, Geneva Tisdale says, "I feel like, sometimes, if a white person had this job, that person would get paid more than me—just because of the color of the skin." Write about your associations with this statement. What does it make you think of? How does it make you feel? What questions would you like to ask Geneva Tisdale if you had a chance to meet her?

B. Pretend that you are Geneva Tisdale and write a letter to the Woolworth's Corporation. Explain how you feel about losing your job after all of this time and what, if anything, you think the company should do to compensate you.

PROJECT ACTIVITY: RESEARCHING THE CIVIL RIGHTS MOVEMENT

What questions do you still have about the Civil Rights Movement? Prepare a list of questions that you would like to have answered. You can start with what you wrote in the Orientation and add any others that have come to you after hearing the broadcast. Take your questions to the library and do some research. An encyclopedia is a good place to start. Look under the headings "Civil Rights Movement" and "King, Martin Luther, Jr." You may do general research, or you can focus on finding out about a specific event, such as the Greensboro sit-in, or a specific figure, such as Rosa Parks or Charlayne Hunter. After you have finished your research, summarize your findings and report them to the class.

"I don't believe in miracles and fate and hope and all that other crap that people try to push down on holidays. Things just don't work out that way. Not in real life."

Photo by Claudette Buelow

12 Cynical Santa

Before Listening

ORIENTATION

Santa Claus is a legendary figure who travels around the world on the night before Christmas leaving gifts for all children who have been good during the year. Test your knowledge about Santa by taking the following quiz. Put a T on the line before each true sentence and put an F before each false sentence. The first two have been done for you.

1. **T** He rides in a sleigh pulled by flying reindeer.

2. **F** He takes the bus to work.

3. _____ He has a workshop at the North Pole where elves make toys.

4. _____ He must have another job to support himself during the rest of the year.

5. _____ He wears an artificial beard and moustache.

6. _____ He is well known for being jolly and saying "ho, ho, ho."

7. _____ He knows which children have been "naughty" and "nice."

8. _____ He stands on street corners for long hours.

9. _____ Children leave out food for him on Christmas Eve.

10. _____ He asks holiday shoppers for donations of money.

Check your answers with your teacher. Each of the sentences that is false for Santa Claus is actually true of the subject of this broadcast, a man known as the Cynical Santa.

VOCABULARY

Read each of the following words or phrases from the broadcast. Then, on the line provided, write yes if it is a word or phrase you normally associate with Christmas, no if it is not. Then explain your response. If you are uncertain of the meaning of any word or phrase, you may use a dictionary. The first one has been done for you.

1. volunteer *Yes. People often volunteer their time to help those in need during the Christmas season.*

2. to be "down on one's luck" _____

3. charity _____

4. cynical _____

5. a donation box _____

6. miracles _____

7. hard knocks _____

8. serenade _____

9. etiquette _____

Listening and Understanding

INTRODUCTION

This is an unusual Christmas story. This broadcast is not about the legendary Santa Claus but about the kind of Santa who stands on a corner during the Christmas season, ringing a bell and asking for donations to charity. This particular charity Santa has a nickname. They call him the Cynical Santa. David Isay spent a day with Cynical Santa and learned about his unique approach to his job.

FIRST LISTENING: PREDICTING

Based on the introduction, and his nickname, how do you think Cynical Santa will be different from other charity Santas? Write your prediction on the lines provided below.

_____

_____

_____

_____

Listen to the broadcast to check on your prediction. Don't worry about understanding everything in the story. You'll have a chance to hear it again.

LISTENING FOR COMPREHENSION

Read over the following questions and see whether there are any you can answer from your first listening. Then listen to the broadcast again to check your answers and to find the answers to the remaining questions.

1. What organization does Eddie Sirwinski work for? _____

2. How long has he worked as a Santa? _____

3. Has Eddie Sirwinski had an easy life? Explain. _____

_____

4. What kind of work does he do the rest of the year? _____

_____

5. Why does Eddie Sirwinski find mornings the most difficult part of the day?

_____

_____

6. What is the one-day record for donations? Who holds it? _____

_____

7. Why does Eddie Sirwinski say that he is so successful as a Santa?

_____

8. Is Eddie having a good day? Explain._____

_____

LANGUAGE FOCUS A: NEGATIVE EXPRESSIONS

Sometimes a meaning can best be expressed through a negative expression. By stating what something is not, a negative expression makes it clear that the opposite is then true. Note how David Isay describes Eddie Sirwinski near the beginning of the broadcast.

> *Not your typical* Kris Kringle, he prefers to be known as the Cynical Santa.

The italicized expression means that Cynical Santa is "quite different from the average." ("Kris Kringle" is another name for Santa Claus.)

Read each of the following sentences from the broadcast, noting the italicized negative expression. Then find the positive expression below which means the same thing. Write the letter next to the definition in the space provided. The first one has been done for you.

___d___ 1. It's *not hard to pick out* Cynical Santa from all of the others.

_____ 2. I'm *not* here *to entertain people*.

_____ 3. Although etiquette lessons are given in Santa School, Eddie Sirwinski says he's *never taken* them *too seriously*.

_____ 4. *Despite his unorthodox methods*, Santa Sirwinski is the all-time greatest money maker in the history of the Volunteers of America.

_____5. "New Yorkers are cynical people. They kind of know that I'm *not a bullshit artist*."

_____6. There are the *countless times* he's been kicked and sworn at and spit on.

_____7. Things are *not looking rosy*.

_____8. It's getting colder and colder. But *that doesn't faze Sirwinski a bit*.

a. (I'm here) for a serious purpose; in order to do my job
b. Sirwinski maintains the same attitude
c. many, many occasions
d. easy to spot or identify
e. paid little attention to; ignored
f. (appearing to be) very difficult
g. although he is very different from others
h. a sincere and truthful person

Listening for Analysis

Listen to the broadcast again to answer the following questions. As you listen, follow along with the transcript and underline passages that provide support for your answers. You can also mark any places where the meaning of the broadcast is unclear and ask your teacher for an explanation.

1. What parts of the broadcast show Eddie Sirwinski's cynicism or negative attitude?

_____

_____

_____

_____

2. Are there any ways in which he is *not* cynical? At what parts of the broadcast does he seem sweet or even hopeful?

_____

_____

3. Do you think this broadcast is funny? If so, what parts make you laugh? If not, what is your reaction to this broadcast?

_____

_____

LANGUAGE FOCUS B: POLITE AND IMPOLITE LANGUAGE

One way in which Cynical Santa is different from most charity Santas in that he often uses impolite language. Eddie Sirwinski often either uses "swear words," such as "hell," "damn," and "bullshit," or talks in a way that is too direct to be considered polite.

For example, when people at the center say "See ya later" and "See you down the road" as Eddie Sirwinski leaves for work, he replies "Maybe" and grunts. A more polite response would be to say "See you later," "Goodbye," or to make some other positive response.

A. Look through the tapescript to find at least five more examples of impolite language. Write each one in the left-hand column of the chart below. In the right-hand column, write a more polite way of expressing this idea, if possible. If there is no polite way to express it, then simply explain what the impolite expression means.

Impolite Expression	Polite Expression (or Meaning)
1. . . . all that other crap.	1. Other things like that.
2.	2.
3.	3.
4.	4.
5.	5.

B. With your group, briefly discuss the following questions. Which of these impolite expressions, if any, do you think you would ever want to use? In what situation might you use each? What are the advantages and disadvantages of using impolite expressions in a second language?

After Listening

DISCUSSION ACTIVITIES

With your group, choose one of the following activities.

A. Toward the end of the story, David Isay refers to Cynical Santa's "unique Santa Philosophy." How would you describe Eddie Sirwinski's "philosophy"? How do you think his personal experiences have influenced his way of seeing the world? Give examples from the tapescript. How is his approach to life similar to or different from yours?

B. Do you think that Americans are generally polite? Explain how you feel the behavior of Americans, in general, compares with that which is expected in your culture. Do you see Americans as being too direct? As too indirect? Give examples either from your personal contact with Americans or from what you've picked up from the media. (And remember that Cynical Santa is not exactly a typical American.)

WRITING ACTIVITIES

Choose one of the following topics.

A. Many people in the United States complain that the Christmas season is insincere and too commercial. Write a brief essay in which you express your point of view about how either Christmas or another holiday is celebrated in your home country. Include a personal story from your own experience that shows why you feel the way you do about this holiday and the way it is celebrated.

B. There is a proverb that says, "A cynic is a person who knows the price of everything and the value of nothing." Write an essay relating this proverb to Cynical Santa. First, express the meaning of this proverb in your own words. Then, based on the meaning of the proverb, explain why you think Eddie Sirwinski is or is not a cynical person. Support your opinion by giving examples from the broadcast.

PROJECT ACTIVITY: MAKING YOUR OWN DOCUMENTARY

Pick a person or topic you find interesting and create your own documentary. Start by choosing a topic that you would like to learn more about and that relates in some way to American culture. Then do all the background research you can on your topic in the library and on the phone. When you are ready, set out into the field to interview people who are directly involved. To record your interviews, you may use an audio tape recorder (as David Isay does), you may use a video recorder, or you may simply take notes.

If you choose to make an audio recording, consider the advice from David Isay on the next page.

When you have gathered enough information, put the story into a presentable form. You may not be able to edit as professionally as David Isay does, but you can introduce your subject in your own words and then tell the story with a combination of your narration and the quotes you have on tape or in your notebook. When your project is ready, present it to the class. You may work individually or in a group.

How to Make Broadcast-Quality Recordings

General Rules

- Try to record interviews in the quietest possible place and one with no echo. A living room or bedroom with lots of carpeting and the door shut is good; restaurants are a terrible place to record. Turn off all radios and anything else that is making noise.

- When you're trying to decide where to do the interview, you might want to tell your subject something like, "The room doesn't have to look nice, it just has to sound nice."

- Put the microphone about five inches away from your subject's mouth. Place the microphone slightly off axis to the center of the talker's mouth to avoid "plosives" (that is, loud "P" sounds that distort).

- Think like you're making a movie—think in terms of scenes, sound elements, and transitions.

- Always bring extra batteries and extra blank tapes.

The Interview

- Start by having the subjects identify themselves. Ask, "Who are you? How old are you? What do you do? How long have you been doing it?"

- Stories with a lot of emotional content work very well on radio. Questions like "How does this make you feel?" and so forth tend to yield good responses.

- For visually descriptive information, ask your subject to "paint a picture" with words of whatever you are asking them to describe.

- Take careful notes about how people/things look (you can either write them down or speak them into tape recorder) for possible inclusion in the radio script.

- Be absolutely silent when your subject is talking. Don't laugh when someone is talking. Never say "uh huh." Don't interrupt.

- If some noise interrupts you, just stop and let it pass. If you're in the middle of something important, let your subjects finish speaking and then have them repeat what they've said.

Adapted from The Public Radio Writers Project/Sound Portraits Productions, Inc., © 1997.

Answers

Chapter 1 Hunan Chef

BEFORE LISTENING

ORIENTATION

Responses will vary.

VOCABULARY

1. famished
2. savor
3. carafe
4. sliced; diced
5. complimentary
6. leftovers
7. sip
8. to settle the bill; to pay the check
9. to pick up the tab

Listening and Understanding

First Listening: Predicting

1. It serves Chinese food.
2. The rent has been raised, and David Ma cannot afford to pay it.
3. Crispy Orange Chicken costs $7.50.

Listening for Comprehension

1. He has been eating there regularly since his freshman year of college, nine years ago.
2. He usually eats there on Monday nights.
3. He immediately hurried over to Hunan Chef.
4. Joe, his friend, told David that he was getting married.
5. The owner invited David to come to his home to eat.
6. He says it was "outstanding and consistent."
7. Yes. Once he had ordered diced chicken with peanuts and hot pepper sauce but by mistake was given sliced chicken. David was so upset by the mistake that he couldn't eat the sliced chicken.
8. He didn't pay anything. The owner wouldn't let him pay.

Language Focus A: Phrasal Verbs (1)

Exercise A

1. d
2. c
3. b
4. h
5. e
6. f
7. a
8. g

Exercise B

1. up
2. in
3. up
4. down
5. up
6. out
7. up

8. on
9. up
10. off

Listening for Analysis

Responses will vary. Some sample responses are given.

1. David Isay can be seen as a loyal and dedicated friend (as shown by the fact that he rushes over on hearing the bad news) but also quite fixed in his ways and a bit conservative (as shown by how inflexible his eating habits are).
2. David Ma can be seen as a warm and generous person (as shown by his invitation to David to eat at his house, and his "tearful goodbye" to the dishwasher).
3. Responses will vary.
4. Many listeners find this to be a bittersweet story, one that is both sad and happy, because the warmth of the friendship is mixed with sadness that this period is coming to an end.

Language Focus B: Vocabulary in Context (1)

1. g
2. c
3. a
4. b
5. h
6. f
7. d
8. e

AFTER LISTENING

Responses to all activities will vary.

Chapter 2 The Nixie Clerk

BEFORE LISTENING

ORIENTATION

1. yes
2. no
3. yes

4. yes

5. yes

6. yes

7. yes

8. no

VOCABULARY

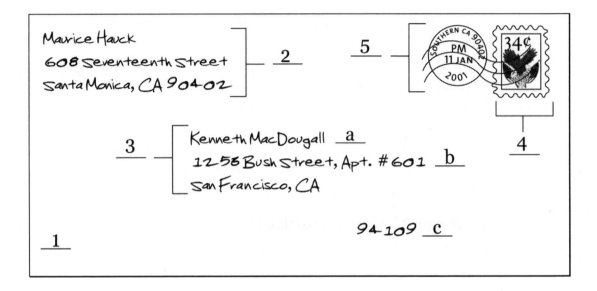

LISTENING AND UNDERSTANDING

First Listening: Predicting

Answers will vary.

Listening for Comprehension

1. It is a very large room with high ceilings and is broken up into different work areas.

2. When a sorting clerk can't read an envelope, he or she hits a reject button, which sends the envelope to a nixie clerk.

3. No. He is able to read most of them very quickly.

4. They include the names of Abigail Van Buren and Sigmund Freud, a footprint, and "occupant Roxette."

5. a, c, d

6. They are returned to the sender, if possible; if not, they go to a "dead letters" office, where they are opened.

7. About 3,000.

8. He feels tired but is satisfied that his work has been helpful to others.

Language Focus A: Nonsexist Language

Exercise A

1. police officer
2. flight attendant
3. firefighter
4. salesperson, sales representative
5. house cleaner, office cleaner, housekeeper
6. chair, chairperson
7. homemaker
8. businessperson (or, more specifically, business executive, manager, retailer, entrepreneur, etc.)

Exercise B

Responses may vary. Some sample responses are given.

1. Replace "man" with "person" or "individual."
2. Replace "working man" with "worker" or "wage earner."
3. Replace "man and wife" with "husband and wife."
4. Replace "mankind" with "humankind," "society," "the human species" etc.

Note: Sentences 5 and 6 raise the question of "generic he," which is one of the most difficult to solve. Some possible responses are given.

5. Every student should try to do his or her best. All students should try to do their best.

In speech, but not writing, the following is often used and accepted:
    Each student should try to do their best.
6. When a reporter covers a controversy, he or she has a responsibility to be fair to all sides.

    When reporters cover a controversy, they have a responsibility to be fair to all sides.

    When covering a controversy, a reporter has a responsibility to be fair to all sides.

    When a controversy is covered, there is a responsibility to be fair to all sides.

Listening for Analysis

Responses will vary. Some sample responses are given

1. "It's a battle . . . it's me and the letter. And I know there's a address in there and I'm looking at it . . . saying, 'You're not going to beat me'" (lines 75–79); "Sometimes, I put a letter down and two or three minutes later it'll hit me . . . and I'll look at it again and I'll say, 'That's it'" (lines 120–125).

2. "If we can't figure out where your letter was supposed to go, that's it. We consider ourselves the best" (lines 31–34); "The mind is shot, the eyes are gone, but I feel good because I know I got some people their mail" (lines 157–159). This passage might also be used as evidence of item 1.

3. "I got this . . . Bingo, love it like that! Yes!" (lines 65–66); "OK, yes, yes. . . . Going to grandma. . . . Is that right? Washington, yeah" (lines 170–173).

4. Al asks about Sigmund Freud, "I don't know, does he still receive mail?" (lines 100–101); Al also offers help in a good-natured way when David tries to read an address (lines 135–140).

Language Focus B: Describing a Process with Vivid Simple Present Verbs

A. draws, rewrites, whisks; holds . . . up, freezes, scratches, makes a face, massages.

B. Responses will vary.

AFTER LISTENING

Responses to all activities will vary.

Chapter 3 Airplane Ashes

BEFORE LISTENING

ORIENTATION

Responses will vary.

VOCABULARY

1. a. cremation; b. burial; c. funeral
2. a. casket; b. urn; c. oatmeal box
3. a. mourners; b. pilot
4. a. pilot; b. oatmeal box

LISTENING AND UNDERSTANDING

First Listening: Predicting

1. Responses will vary.
2. He uses the oatmeal box to hold the ashes, which he then scatters them from his plane.

Listening for Comprehension

1. He's called the "pilot of death." This name does not seem to fit him because he is quite cheerful and friendly.
2. It is more personal than other kinds of funerals. Dick Falk also claims that if the ashes are caught in the jet stream they will continue to fly forever.
3. They are mailed to him.
4. name: Mabel; occupation: secretary; hometown: St. Louis; age: 82 years old; destination: over the Statue of Liberty
5. They look like gray sand.
6. $250.00
7. No. He used to get a few jobs per week; now he gets one per month or fewer.
8. Dick Falk wants his own ashes to be scattered along 42nd Street in New York City.

Language Focus A: Parts of the Body Used as Verbs

1. hand
2. elbow
3. thumbed
4. footing
5. nosing
6. eyeing
7. shoulder
8. mouthed

Listening for Analysis

Responses will vary. Some sample responses are given.

1. People are usually much more serious and respectful in talking about death.
2. Both the words themselves and the enthusiasm in Dick Falk's voice make him sound eccentric.

Other places that reveal Dick Falk's eccentricity include:

  a. how he describes the impersonality of other services;

  b. that he talks to the ashes;

  c. that he uses an oatmeal box to carry the ashes;

  d. that he seems so fascinated with the lives of his clients;

  e. that he recites poetry while scattering the ashes;

  f. the very unlikely story he tells about the ashes staying in the jet stream permanently.

Language Focus B: Sequence Words

Exercise A

1. "Actually" is not a sequence word. Dick Falk uses it to call attention to the fact that what he is about to say is somewhat unusual.

2. then; finally

Exercise B

a. First

b. Next / Then

c. Then / Next

d. Actually

e. In the afternoon

f. Finally

Exercise C

Responses will vary.

AFTER LISTENING

Responses to all activities will vary.

Chapter 4 **Chained Girl**

BEFORE LISTENING

ORIENTATION

1. This proverb means that physical punishment is a necessary part of raising a child well. Responses to items 2, 3, and 4 will vary.

VOCABULARY

1. i
2. h
3. e
4. c
5. b
6. a
7. g
8. f
9. d

LISTENING AND UNDERSTANDING

First Listening: Predicting

Responses will vary.

Listening for Comprehension

1. They live in the South Bronx, a poor neighborhood with drug and crime problems.
2. She was twelve years old. She began using crack cocaine and then stopped going to school and began staying away from home.
3. They were not able to get any help. They were "given the run-around."
4. She could reach most of the rooms in the apartment. She was able to watch television and see visitors.
5. They would leave keys to Linda's chains with a neighbor in case of fire.
6. Yes. They were arrested and held in jail for two days before being released.
7. She left home again and was found in a crack house (a place where people buy and take crack cocaine).
8. She has been offered a place in a drug rehabilitation facility.

Language Focus A: Preposition Combinations

1. chained to
2. were upset by
3. was addicted to
4. search for
5. appealed to
6. prevents . . . from
7. disappeared from
8. growing . . . angry with

9. care for
10. putting . . . through
11. worry about

Listening for Analysis
Responses will vary.

Language Focus B: Features of Spoken Language
Exercise A
1. "It was a very comfortable situation."
2. "I mean" draws the listeners' attention to what will be said next; "you know what I mean?" asks for the listener to signal understanding.
3. Responses will vary.
4. The sentence would probably be reduced to simply, "It was a very comfortable situation."

Exercise B
Responses will vary.

AFTER LISTENING

Responses to all activities will vary.

Chapter 5 Senior DJs

BEFORE LISTENING

ORIENTATION

Responses will vary.

VOCABULARY

The age words should be arranged in the order shown in the chart below. Ranges of years may vary somewhat; the responses shown in the chart are typical.

Age Word	Range of Years
infant	0–1
toddler	2–3
child	0–17
adolescent	13–19
adult	18 and up
middle-aged person	40–65
senior citizen	65 and up

LISTENING AND UNDERSTANDING

First Listening: Predicting

Responses will vary.

Listening for Comprehension

1. It takes place in the community room of a senior center.
2. The Shurrs do it themselves.
3. They couldn't find a place that played the kind of music they enjoyed, so they decided to provide it themselves.
4. No. At first, no one is dancing, and some people seem bored or upset.
5. He uses a variety of music, mixing it up every few songs.
6. They use old-fashioned, low-tech equipment: a record player, a tape recorder, and portable speakers.
7. They dislike today's pop music, particularly Madonna or 2 Live Crew. They disagree about the lambada, which Estelle likes but Meyer doesn't.
8. They enjoy playing music, and they find that it makes them feel better physically. It helps them forget their aches and pains.

Language Focus A: Using Descriptive Adverbs

Exercise A

1. d; "make their way"
2. b; "lays out"
3. f; the entire sentence.
4. a; "are tapping their fingers"

5. h; "motion"

6. g; "nod and wink at each other"

7. c; "low-tech"

8. e; the entire sentence.

Exercise B

1. slow

2. slowly; carefully

3. knowing

4. impatient; meticulously

5. well; good

Listening for Analysis

Responses will vary. The following are sample responses.

Signs that the Shurrs are senior citizens.	Signs that the Shurrs remain "young at heart."
They are "white haired and a little pudgy" and wear "thick eyeglasses."	They carry in and set up the equipment in themselves.
Their equipment is old and out-of-date.	They "aren't fazed at all" when the dance gets off to a slow start.
They don't like much of today's pop music.	Before long, "the floor is crammed with dozens of couples"
They have health problems, both serious and minor.	Meyer says that he "could go a couple of more hours."

Language Focus B: Using "Will" and "Going To"

Exercise A

1. I'll help

2. I'm going to

3. I'll go

4. I'll switch; I'm only going to be here

5. I'm going to have dinner; we're going to go; I'll probably stay home

Exercises B

Responses will vary.

Exercise C

Responses will vary.

AFTER LISTENING

Responses to all activities will vary.

Chapter 6 Advance Obituaries

BEFORE LISTENING

ORIENTATION

Responses will vary.

VOCABULARY

1. e
2. g
3. b
4. i
5. a
6. h
7. d
8. f
9. j
10. c

LISTENING AND UNDERSTANDING

First Listening: Predicting

Responses will vary.

Listening for Comprehension

1. The large room is quiet and neatly organized. No, it used to be much wilder.
2. They want to do a more thorough job than can be done in a few hours "on deadline."

3. He relies on his wife's intuitive suggestions.

4. She makes an appointment to interview them.

5. He finds that people are uncomfortable about the idea of being interviewed for their own obituary.

6. No one is allowed to see his or her own advance obituary (not even the publisher of the *New York Times*).

7. He takes a great deal of pride in his work.

8. Fonda was an actor. He was famous for film and stage appearances. He usually played honest, dignified characters.

Language Focus A: Past Tense Verbs in Context

Exercise A

1. exemplified
2. died
3. was
4. retained
5. was enhanced
6. was expressed
7. was
8. enjoyed
9. lived
10. existed
11. remarked
12. project (The simple present is used because Fonda's words are being quoted directly.)
13. tries (The same reason as in item 12.)
14. is survived (The simple present is used because this action continues; the people being described are still alive.)

Exercise B

Responses will vary.

Listening for Analysis

Responses will vary; some possible responses are given.

1. He is rather difficult to listen to. He speaks slowly, with much hesitation and many speech errors. However, he speaks carefully and chooses his words thoughtfully.

2. In contrast to his speech, his is writing style is concise, efficient, and perhaps even elegant. In both speech and writing, he seems very thoughtful and very careful with language.
3. Responses will vary.

Language Focus B: Using the Passive Voice

Exercise A

Responses will vary. Sample responses are given.

1. In one cabinet, Peter Flint keeps the advance obits that *are being edited*. (Reason: The passive keeps the focus on Peter Flint, rather than the editors.)
2. These are the ones that he *may be called on* to answer questions on. (Reason: The same as for number 1.)
3. Once a client *is chosen,* the writers will take anything from two days to a number of weeks to compose the obituary. (Reason: It is unimportant who chooses the client, as the focus is being shifted to the act of writing.)
4. In four locked drawers *are stored* the hundreds of advance obituaries . . . which Peter Flint has written. (Reason: It is unimportant who has stored the obituaries.)
5. No one *is permitted* to see his or her own obituary. (Reason: It is unclear/unimportant who is not permitting people to see their own obituaries.)
6. Besides his wife and children, [Henry Fonda] *is survived* by four grandchildren and a sister . . . (Reason: The passive voice keeps the focus on Fonda.)
7. In lieu of flowers, contributions *may be made* to the Henry Fonda Theater Center Memorial . . . (Reason: It is unclear/unimportant who will be making contributions.)

Exercise B

1. For the sake of good taste, the names of advance obituary "clients" *are kept* confidential (by the Times).
2. X (No passive form is possible.)
3. From two days to a number of weeks *will be taken* (by the writers) to compose an obituary.
4. X (No passive form is possible.)
5. Pride *is taken* (by the obituary writers) in ensuring that important figures *are given* the farewell they deserve.

AFTER LISTENING

Responses to all activities will vary.

Chapter 7 Diaryman

BEFORE LISTENING

ORIENTATION

Responses will vary.

VOCABULARY

1. b
2. a
3. e
4. f
5. i
6. g
7. h
8. c
9. d

LISTENING AND UNDERSTANDING

First Listening: Predicting
Responses will vary.

Listening for Comprehension

Exercise A
Responses will vary. A sample response follows.

His Family:	What He Eats:
	canned salmon and orange juice for lunch
	cookies and milk later in the afternoon

The Weather:	His Feelings:
reports the temperature in various locations at certain times	
says nothing about what it's like outside	

Prices:	Miscellaneous:
complains about the price of meat	the weight of the newspaper news reports He actually puts some things into the diary — price stickers, nasal hair

Exercise B

Responses will vary. Sample responses follow.

1. He tends to focus on small details and things that can be precisely measured.
2. He does not talk at all about emotions, or feelings.
3. David Isay reverses the usual order of these words to imply that, for Robert Shields, writing about what he does has become more important than actually living his life.

Language Focus A: Units of Measure

Exercise A

1. d
2. a
3. f
4. c
5. b
6. g
7. e

Exercise B

1. 11″ × 14″ (pronounced "eleven inches by fourteen inches")
2. 1 lb., 11½ oz. ("one pound, eleven and a half ounces")
3. 222 w.p.m. ("two hundred twenty-two words per minute")
4. ½ doz. ("half a dozen" or "one half-dozen")
5. 2 c. ("two cups")
6. 20¢ per lb. ("twenty cents per pound" or "twenty cents a pound")
7. 56° ("fifty-six degrees")
8. 51° ("fifty-one degrees")

Listening for Analysis

Responses will vary.

Language Focus B: Vocabulary in Context (2)

1. c
2. f.
3. i.
4. b
5. j.
6. a
7. h

8. e
9. d
10. g

AFTER LISTENING

Responses to all activities will vary.

Chapter 8 **Passover Wine**

BEFORE LISTENING

ORIENTATION

Responses will vary.

VOCABULARY

1. i
2. e
3. a
4. f
5. d
6. g
7. h
8. b
9. j
10. c

LISTENING AND UNDERSTANDING

First Listening: Predicting
Responses will vary.

Listening for Comprehension
1. The building is old and in poor shape. Inside, the store is very crowded.
2. They have been open since 1899. They have never stopped selling wine. During the period of Prohibition, they stayed open with a government license to make wine for religious purposes.

3. For many years the wine was made entirely at the store. Today, the grapes are grown and crushed in upstate New York, but the wine is still fermented in the cellar of the store.
4. Most of them say that coming to Schapiro's is a tradition for them. One man also likes the fact that the wine is made at the store.
5. She is very friendly and outgoing, and somewhat loud.
6. The most visited spot is the tasting table, where customers can drink small cups of the wine for free.
7. Passover wine reminds him of Seders from his youth and the first two times he got drunk. (The second time, he embarrassed his family by telling secrets at the dinner table.)
8. No, Schapiro's may not have as many customers in the store, but it is doing a good wholesale trade, and the children will take over the business.

Language Focus A: Using "Would" and "Used To"

Exercise A
1. used to live
2. used to do/would do
3. used to speak
4. used to bargain/would bargain
5. used to be
6. used to eat/would eat
7. used to see/would see
8. used to talk/would talk
9. used to help/would help

Exercise B
Responses will vary.

Listening for Analysis
Responses to all items will vary. Sample responses to items 1 and 2 follow.

1. a. Linda greets everyone informally. She says, "Some of my customers are so cute."
   b. A customer asks Linda a question about another store in the neighborhood.
   c. Customers linger at the sampling table.
   d. Customers sing.
   e. Linda asks David to sample some wine. She asks him whether he is married.

f. A customer teases Linda. He says, "All the time, when I come here, she's right here by the cash register. She always takes my money, but she never overcharges."

2. At the end, there is a more formal exchange between Linda and a customer named Hocksameyer. However, it is not clear if they are being serious or are kidding around.

3. Responses will vary.

Language Focus B: Using the Passive Voice to Describe a Process

Exercise A

1. are picked
2. (are) packed
3. are loaded
4. transport
5. are peeled
6. (are) cored
7. remains
8. is cooked
9. (is) blended
10. changes
11. is packed
12. move
13. are labeled
14. are loaded
15. (are) shipped

Exercise B

Responses will vary.

AFTER LISTENING

Responses to all activities will vary.

Chapter 9 The Joe Franklin Show

BEFORE LISTENING

ORIENTATION

Responses will vary.

VOCABULARY

Exercise A

Responses will vary. Some sample responses are given.

1. A cartoon features animated, rather than live-action, characters. This category can include both children's fare, such as "Scooby-Doo" and "The Flintstones," and cartoons for a general audience, such as "The Simpsons."
2. Soap operas are melodramatic serials traditionally broadcast in the middle of the day, such as "Days of Our Lives" and "General Hospital." The category can also include such prime-time "soaps" as "Melrose Place."
3. Talk shows generally feature a host who interviews celebrities or other interesting people. They include "The Oprah Winfrey Show," "The Tonight Show," and "The Late Show with David Letterman."
4. News shows include local, national, and international news. Today, there are also twenty-four-hour news channels, such as CNN.
5. A sitcom is a half-hour situation comedy. Classic sitcoms include "All in the Family," "Cheers," and "Seinfeld."
6. Dramas are one hour and serious in content. Popular dramas include "E.R.," "NYPD Blue," and "Murder, She Wrote."
7. A miniseries is shown for a number of hours over a limited time—one to several weeks. It is often an historical epic, such as "Roots" or "North and South."

Exercise B

Responses will vary.

LISTENING AND UNDERSTANDING

First Listening: Predicting

Responses will vary.

Listening for Comprehension

1. a. 1,000
   b. 40
   c. 28,000
   d. 250,000
2. No. The people at the TV station didn't think Joe's idea was visual enough.

3. He acts very relaxed, paying bills, reading notes, etc. He does not seem nervous.
4. He gives long, detailed, and somewhat exaggerated introductions.
5. Joe says the key has been his sincerity; he doesn't make fun of his guests or talk down to his audience.
6. Yes. For example, he promotes the musician's cassette tape.
7. Joe has no plans to retire. He intends to do thousands more shows.
8. He is in a good mood and full of energy.

Language Focus A: Groups of Synonyms

Exercise A
1. d
2. a
3. f
4. c
5. e
6. b

Exercise B
Responses will vary.

Listening for Analysis
Responses will vary. Some sample responses follow.

1. Joe seems to be stretching the truth at the following points in the story:
   a. when he says he gets a thousand calls a day;
   b. when he says the phone actually explodes;
   c. in the introductions he gives to his guests (his guests are probably not as well known as he says they are);
   d. when he says the musician's cassette is doing well.
   The claims themselves certainly seem unlikely. Also, Joe's tone of voice is very excited; he often sounds more like a salesman than a reporter. This makes what he says seem suspicious.
2. David Isay says, "There's a lot that's hard to believe about Joe Franklin." David also uses indirect speech every time he presents one of Joe's claims (e.g., "Joe Franklin says that . . . ").

Language Focus B: The Language of Hype

Exercise A

1. Responses will vary. Sample responses follow.
    a. "Dan, I need you maniacally, pathologically."
    b. "Put it on the critical list, critical."
    c. " . . . give me a buzz on Friday morning, I'll make you happy."
2. Responses will vary. Sample responses follow.
    a. "They are the top comedy team of their time . . . "
    b. "Everybody wants to chat with America's best-known, best-loved . . . "
    c. " . . . a most respected biotechnologist . . . "

Exercise B

1. tornado-stricken
2. unfailingly entertaining

Exercise C

Responses will vary.

AFTER LISTENING

Responses to all activities will vary.

Chapter 10 **Kipperman's Pawnshop and Wedding Chapel**

BEFORE LISTENING

ORIENTATION

Responses will vary. Possible responses follow.

People: bride, bridegroom, maid of honor, best man

Events: engagement party, bridal shower, bachelor party, rehearsal dinner, ceremony, reception

Things: wedding rings, wedding cake, bouquet

VOCABULARY

Exercise A

1. f
2. i
3. j
4. a
5. c
6. e
7. h
8. b
9. g
10. d

Exercise B

Responses may vary. Items that typically have spiritual or religious associations are wedding chapel; to be ordained; newlyweds; divine inspiration; and stained-glass windows. Items that often have nonspiritual or profane associations are a pawnshop; to hock; an annulment; a penitentiary; and a divorce.

LISTENING AND UNDERSTANDING

First Listening: Predicting

Responses will vary.

Listening for Comprehension

1. It's very colorful and has eye-catching signs.
2. TVs, VCRs, toasters, tools, jewelry, guns.
3. He had extra wedding rings in his pawnshop, and he didn't want to melt them down.
4. The "buy a ring, get a free wedding" offer appealed to them.
5. They don't take any of the extras, turning down the bouquet, the wedding gown rental, and the videotaping service.
6. No, he says his weddings are "for better or for worse," meaning that they should not be ended just because the couple encounters difficulties.
7. Because Michael is in prison, the wedding must be conducted over the phone.
8. David Isay acts as a stand-in, replacing Michael in the ceremony.

Language Focus A: Phrasal Verbs (2)

1. stand out
   a. 1
   b. 2
2. come in
   a. 1
   b. 3
   c. 2
3. pass on
   a. 2
   b. 1
4. come out
   a. 1
   b. 3
   c. 2
5. pick up
   a. 2
   b. 5
   c. 6
   d. 3
   e. 1
   f. 4

Listening for Analysis

1. Responses will vary. Some sample responses are given.
   a. There is a mural of Kipperman painted on the outside wall, and a large photo of him inside the chapel.
   b. The chapel is decorated in a gaudy way, with such things as blinking Christmas lights and a large metal heart threaded with plastic flowers.
   c. The champagne glasses used for the toast are plastic and empty; the cake is fake.
   d. Most of the items that are used in the ceremony, such as the organ, are for sale.
2. Responses will vary.
3. Responses will vary.

Language Focus B: Formulaic Language

Exercise A

1. a. It asks the bride whether she is willing to marry the groom and to be a good wife.
   b. "Rosario, do you want to marry Michael? Do you promise to follow all the rules of marriage?"
2. a. It performs the actual act of marrying the groom and bride.
   b. "As a representative of the state and of the church, I now announce that the two of you are married."
3. a. It takes place at the very end of the ceremony.
   b. "Once two people have been married in front of God, no other person should come between them." ("Asunder" is an old-fashioned word meaning "apart.")

Exercise B

Responses will vary. Some possible responses are provided.

1. David Isay describes the $14.95 bouquet as "a $50 value." (line 94)
2. Ted Kipperman says of his videotaping service: "One of my employees does it for, say, $49.95. That's a good deal." (lines 100–102)
3. David Isay says of the chapel's organ that it, "incidentally, can be purchased for a mere $200." (line 123–124)

Each of these expressions encourages the customer to make a purchase because the price is low.

AFTER LISTENING

Responses to all activities will vary.

Chapter 11 **Woolworth's Lunch Counter**

BEFORE LISTENING

ORIENTATION

1. Responses may vary. Some possible answers are given below.
   a. In the 1950s and 1960s.
   b. They included Dr. Martin Luther King, Jr., Rosa Parks, and Malcolm X.

c. The goals were to make available to African-Americans all the rights of citizenship. These included the right to vote, the right to be treated equally by police and courts, and the integration of housing, schools, and public businesses.

2. Responses will vary.

VOCABULARY

1. c
2. g
3. a
4. d
5. b
6. h
7. i
8. f
9. e

LISTENING AND UNDERSTANDING

First Listening: Predicting

Responses will vary.

Listening for Comprehension

1. She has worked there for more than forty years, since she was nineteen years old.
2. They cooked, cleaned, and washed dishes but were not allowed to serve food (this was in addition to not being allowed to eat at the lunch counter).
3. At first she thought they were playing a joke. As she realized they were serious, she became nervous and stayed away from them.
4. The first sit-in lasted six days and was not successful.
5. It was her manager's idea.
6. She ate an egg salad sandwich.
7. She earns $5.50 per hour.
8. She wanted to bring her granddaughter to eat with her at the lunch counter.

Language Focus A: Time Prepositions

1. for
2. in
3. until

4. at

5. at

6. on

7. for

8. in

9. on

10. at

11. since

12. since

13. on

14. until

Listening for Analysis

1a. Geneva expresses pride by saying, "I put myself in my work. Always have," and by listing the variety of jobs she has done (washing glasses, working on the sandwich board, etc.).

b. Geneva seems to have a fond memory of being the first to eat at the lunch counter. (She laughs as she says, "We were the first.")

c. Geneva seems disappointed and perhaps angry in stating her low wage ($5.50 per hour) and in her feeling that she might have been paid more if she were white.

2. Responses will vary.

Language Focus B: Nonstandard English

Exercise A

Responses may vary. Possible responses are given.

1. I've been around. (*or* I have been around.)

2. Take (*or* have) a big bag and anything else.

3. . . . you are shopping. (*or* you're shopping). In more formal English, one might say "As though you are shopping."

4. So we did that.

5. . . . very quickly.

6. a. the photographer and everyone (*or* everybody); b. . . . were in.

Exercise B

Responses will vary.

AFTER LISTENING

Responses to all activities will vary.

BEFORE LISTENING

ORIENTATION

1. T
2. F
3. T
4. F
5. F
6. T
7. T
8. F
9. T
10. F

VOCABULARY

Responses will vary. Sample responses are given.

1. Yes. During the Christmas season people often volunteer their time to help those in need.
2. No. This expression has a negative meaning that conflicts with the spirit of Christmas.
3. Yes. Christmas is a time when many people give money or volunteer their time to charities.
4. No. The spirit of Christmas celebrates hope and innocence, the opposite of cynicism.
5. Yes. Many charities post donation boxes in busy shopping areas so that people will be encouraged to give money.
6. Yes. Christmas is often thought of as a time of miracles, such as the birth of Christ.
7. No. Christmas is a time of idealism, rather than harsh realism.
8. Yes. Singing to others, particularly songs known as Christmas carols, is a seasonal tradition.
9. Yes. Christmas is a time for politeness and thoughtfulness. Observing etiquette is a part of that.

LISTENING AND UNDERSTANDING

First Listening: Predicting

Responses will vary.

Listening for Comprehension

1. Volunteers of America, a charity organization.
2. Seven years.
3. No. He was homeless for ten years and has had trouble with alcoholism.
4. He works sometimes as a welder.
5. He is overrun by schoolchildren.
6. The record is $400, and Eddie holds it.
7. He thinks New Yorkers like him because he is honest and because they too are cynical.
8. No, it has been a long, hard day because he is not receiving many donations and had not been able to take breaks.

Language Focus A: Negative Expressions

1. d
2. a
3. e
4. g
5. h
6. c
7. f
8. b

Listening for Analysis

Responses will vary. Sample responses for items 1 and 2 are given.

1. a. He is generally grumpy and uses a good deal of impolite language (details of which are given in the next exercise); b. He seems particularly negative in saying "I don't believe in miracles and, uh, fate and all that. . . . Things just don't work that way in real life"; c. His "final Christmas message" is "Everybody dies," and he ends by saying "Merry Christmas, Happy Hanukkah, whatever."
2. He seems less cynical when talking to the children (e.g., saying to one, "Hi, sweetheart . . . ").

Language Focus B: Polite and Impolite Expressions

Exercise A

Responses will vary. The following are sample responses.

Impolite Expression	Polite Expression (or Meaning)
1. . . . all that other crap.	Other things like that.
2. Take a walk.	Please leave me alone.
3. I gotta go pee.	Excuse me, I have to go to the restroom.
4. I'm not a bullshit artist.	I can be trusted to tell the truth *or* I won't lie to anyone.
5. To hell with the ho, ho, ho's	(This means that he doesn't want to pretend to be jolly.)
6. It's just a lot of bull.	I don't believe in it.
7. What the hell?	(This expresses disbelief. A milder way of saying it would be, "What the heck?")
8. Whatever.	(This expresses a lack of interest in the subject under discussion.)

Exercise B

Responses will vary.

AFTER LISTENING

Responses to all activities will vary.

Transcripts

Chapter 1 **Hunan Chef**

I've eaten at Hunan Chef religiously since
the first week of my freshman year at
college, nearly nine years ago. Usually
I'm only at the restaurant on Monday
5 nights. I try to keep my visits down to
one a week. But sometimes, when
nothing but the most familiar and
comforting meal will do, I'll call up
Hunan for a delivery.

10   This was one of those nights. I dialed
the number. When the voice on the other
end picked up, I was confused. It was
my friend David, the owner of Hunan
Chef. "David, it's David," I said. "You
don't work tonight. What are you doing 15
there?" There was a pause, and then
David broke the news. This, he told me,
was to be the last night of Hunan Chef. I
threw on a coat and headed over.

    David Ma: Hi, Dave. Oh-oh. 20
    David Isay: Is it . . . is it true?
    DM: I'm sorry, true.
    DI: What, what happened?
    DM: They wanted more rent and we
    cannot afford it. That's it. Sorry, 25
    buddy. I'm going to miss all my
    friends. Take a seat, buddy.

    David leads me to the big round table
in the middle of the restaurant. A table
which, like many others, holds memories 30

for me. This is where my best buddy from college, Joe, and his girlfriend told me they were getting married. David brings over the traditional carafe of complimentary plum wine and we reminisce about our years of Monday night dinners. He tells me that he only recently got word of the rent hike which has put him out of business.

DM: I just find out last week.

DI: Just last week. If I, if I hadn't called tonight, on Monday I would have come here for my weekly meal . . .

DM: Oh, my God, my God, oh no.

DI: . . . and the door would have been shut.

DM: I'm so sorry, buddy. I'm so sorry, really.

DI: What do I do on Monday night? What should I do?

DM: Maybe come my house.

It was not only David that made Hunan Chef special, but also the fare. It was nothing fancy, an all-the-way-standard Chinese menu identical to thousands of others across the country. But the food itself was outstanding and consistent, which is particularly important to someone like me, who has a tendency to order the exact same meal for years on end and does not like unpleasant surprises.

Only once in nine years did Hunan Chef let me down. One night I called in, famished for my diced chicken with peanuts and hot pepper sauce. A few minutes later a buzz at the door and an order of sliced chicken shows up. I just couldn't eat it. That was years ago and the Hunan staff has long since committed my order to memory, but even tonight I feel compelled to make sure that the tragedy is not repeated.

DI: Diced chicken, not sliced. Diced chicken. Diced chicken with peanuts.

Waiter: No problem.

A few minutes later, Mr. Tam, the busboy, who looks something like a Chinese Peter Lorre, emerges from the kitchen with my last supper. I savor it.

After the meal, I wander to the front of the restaurant, where David is bidding a tearful goodbye to his dishwasher, Mr. Wu. David peels a handwritten sign off the restaurant's window which reads "Crispy Orange Chicken $7.50" and hands it to me as a keepsake memento. I head back to the table aching for a message profound and comforting in the fortune cookie which awaits me. Instead it reads, "Simplicity and clarity should be your theme in dress." I take a final sip of plum wine, pick up my bag of leftovers, and walk to the front of the restaurant to settle the bill.

DM: Don't do that.

David insists on picking up the tab.

DM: Money can buy some things, of course it can buy some things. Some things it cannot buy. Like a friend. We talk about it, you know what I'm saying. Keep the memories, buddy. Just a friend.

For National Public Radio, I'm David Isay.

DM: I'll miss you, buddy. I'll miss you, man.

DM: Take care, O.K. Say hello to
Joe, O.K.
DI: O.K.

Chapter 2 **The Nixie Clerk**

On Ninth Avenue in Manhattan, the huge
Morgan Central Mail Facility is the heart
of New York's postal service. It is on the
third floor of this building that the bulk of
New York's letters are sorted, a
cavernous open space with twenty-foot high
ceilings spanning the entire city block. At
one end of the floor, endless rows of
clerks sit at old letter-sorting machines.
Sixty times a minute, a robotic vacuum
arm sucks up a letter and slaps it in front
of the clerks, who punch a button on a
keyboard which shoots the letters into the
appropriate zip code bins.

But every so often a letter will pass by
which the clerks cannot read. And for
those special cases, there is a reject button to
push which causes the letters to fly into
reject bins. Which, when filled, are carted
all the way across the third floor of the
building to an area tucked in the far, far
corner of the room. Here, during the
evening hours when most of the city's
mail is being processed, you'll find five
postal employees struggling through trays
of hard-to-read letters. These are New
York's nixie clerks. The term is old post
office slang for employees who deal with
difficult mail.

Al Flynn: We call ourselves the last
resort. This is it. I mean, if we can't

figure out where your letter was
supposed to go, that's it. We consider
ourselves the best.

Veteran nixie clerk Al Flynn sits at
station number three. Like the rest of the
nixie clerks, Al sits straight up on a bench
surrounded on three sides by rows of
post office box slots. In front of him is a
cardboard tray holding about 800 letters
which he is about to decipher.

AF: Every day I come in here and I
say to myself, "Well let me see what
they have in store for me today, what
kind of, uh, challenge, what kind of
mystery, what kind of game, what
kind of, um, adventure am I going to
find waiting for me today?" And I am
never disappointed.

Al is thin with thick glasses. He wears
untucked postal service blues, holds a
pen in one hand, and picks up letters with
the other.

AF: *Herald Tribune, Herald
Tribune's goin' to 36 . . .*

Al is something else to watch at work,
talking himself through each letter. Most
of the envelopes seem to come to him
instantly. He simply draws a line under
the offending scrawl, rewrites it to the
side, and whisks it into the appropriate
mail slot for delivery.

AF: *This doesn't look like anything
here, c-h, c, c-i, c-h, c-h, yeah, yeah,
OK, I got this. 74 Charlton, C-h-a-r-
l-t-o-n. Bingo, love it like that! YES!*

Every dozen letters or so, though, Al
comes across a toughie. He holds the
envelope up and freezes, staring at it

motionlessly. Then he scratches his chin, makes a face, massages his head. He usually figures it out sooner or later.

AF: *Huh, I gotcha now, I gotcha now . . . a-t-v alright.*

It's a battle, it's a battle. You know, uh, it's me and the letter. And I know there's a address in there and I'm looking at it and I'm saying, "You're not gonna beat me." Someone else would look at it and they'll say, "What the heck is this? It looks like chicken scratch, it looks like a, you know, um, Chinese puzzle," but I know there's a address in there.

Oh, you know what? This could be Greenland. This could be Greenland. Greenland is not in New York, though. And it's not in the U.S.A.

Al deals with all sorts of problem envelopes over the course of a night. Letters with incorrect addresses or no addresses at all. Tonight there's an envelope addressed to former first lady Abigail Van Buren, another being sent to "occupant Roxette," who apparently lives simply, "behind the gate." One envelope just has a big footprint on it. Another is going to Sigmund Freud.

AF: *I don't know, does he still receive mail? Hmm.*

But the majority of Al's time is spent puzzling over bad handwriting, in black pen and blue pen, in pencil and crayon. Some of the addresses start out neat enough and then disintegrate into a jumble. Others are illegible all the way through.

AF: *Look like it says "unmask" or "oon-misk." Very difficult, very difficult. Very frustrating.*

Al uses a variety of tricks to puzzle out hieroglyphic handwriting, like identifying one letter—say the N in "New York"—and then finding all of the other Ns on the envelope. He matches and eliminates and sounds it out. Most of all, he says, he uses imagination and a lot of patience.

AF: Sometimes, I put a letter down and two or three minutes later it'll hit me what they was trying to say or what they meant to say, and I'll go back to the letter and I'll look at it again and I'll say, "That's it."

David Isay: Can we look at some letters together?

AF: Sure we can.

DI: OK, now this one looks to me, and I'm not an expert . . .

AF: OK.

DI: . . . but I read on this letter, "Margaret Sandwich Schlep." Is that what you see?

AF: Um, you're, you're pretty close. It looks like either "Margaret" or "Ma pot." Sandwich, you had the cor—, the second word correct, but that, I think that last word is "shop" s-h-o-p. Or ship. But if, uh . . .

There are some letters that Al Flynn just can't figure out. If the letter has a return address, it's returned to sender. In worst-case scenarios, if there's no return address or if the return address is unreadable, Al forwards the envelope to the dead letters office, where postal workers have the authority to open it up and try to figure out where it came from.

150 AF: *Ris-, risbee, risbay . . . yeah.*

Over the course of a single shift, Al Flynn will struggle through something like 3,000 letters. That is no small task. By the end of the evening, Flynn says

155 that he is pretty well incapacitated by his night of handwriting hell.

AF: The mind is shot, the eyes are gone, but I feel good because I know I got some people their mail that really

160 had no possible chance of getting their letters. And I know somewhere along the line, whenever that person gets that letter, they'll be happy. Especially when they look at the

165 address and say, How in the world did I get this?

Now you know. Al Flynn is a nixie clerk at the Morgan Central Mail Facility in Manhattan.

170 AF: *OK, yes, yes. Yes, going to grandma, grandma Runyon. Six Washington Avenue? Is that right? Washington, yeah.*

For National Public Radio, I'm David

175 Isay.

AF: *I got it again. I love it, I tell you.*

Chapter 3 **Airplane Ashes**

It's a sunny Wednesday afternoon at Teterboro Airport just outside of Manhattan and Dick Falk has settled comfortably into the copilot spot of a

5 Cessna four-seater. Although he may be known as the Pilot of Death, Falk does not look nearly as intimidating as his title might suggest. He's a smiling, almost bald seventy-nine-year-old in a worn pin-

10 striped suit, with a snow-white goatee and a long handlebar mustache.

Uh, Teterboro tower, Cessna N52491 over to 24 . . . Roger.

For years now, Dick Falk has been

15 scattering people's cremated remains over New York. It is, he says, the only logical way to go. Funerals, after all, are just too expensive. Cremation is great, but what to do with the ashes? Keeping them in an

20 urn on the mantelpiece is just asking for trouble.

Dick Falk: Every now and then, an urn will fall down and break and the ashes go all over the floor. Now you

25 don't want to pick up your husband in a vacuum cleaner, which you'd have to do because you'd never get it out of the rug.

And, he says, just leaving the ashes with the crematorium isn't the answer.

30 DF: They take the ashes and they get a boat maybe and they go out with like maybe five hundred little containers and they take a boat maybe out beyond the twelve-mile limit and

35 then throw the whole darn thing overboard. It's, uh, nothing, uh, sensitive about it at all. They throw them away!

No, not Dick Falk. He disposes his

40 ashes with a distinctly personal touch.

DF: I actually talk to the ashes and, uh, I have a, a feeling for them. I make a, uh, it's a ritual, a ritual of life

45 and death. I'm alive, they're gone!
And, uh, that's what makes it
interesting.

This is Teterboro Airport information . . .

After two decades in the business, Falk
50 has got this ritual down pat. First the
crematorium sends the ashes to his Forty-
Second Street office.

DF: The mailmen bring them to me.
They say, "Falk, you got another
55 one."

Then he carefully transfers the ashes
from the cremator's plain packaging to a
more suitable receptacle.

DF: Actually, I put them in what is
60 known as an oatmeal box because it
fits.

Then, onto the top of this box, Falk
scrawls the deceased client's name and
vital information: his or her one-time
65 profession, age at the time of death,
hometown. Falk rents a plane and a pilot,
and off they go.

Tower, cleared for takeoff 52491 . . .

Today, Falk is toting an oatmeal box
70 holding a woman named Mabel. Mabel,
according to the top of the box, was from
St. Louis. She was a secretary and she
died at the age of eighty-two. Now she's
headed towards the Statue of Liberty. All
75 of Dick Falk's clients specify that special
place in their lives that they want to be
sprinkled over. Falk says the statue is his
most frequently requested target, ahead of
Coney Island, the Catskills, Asbury
80 Park, Atlantic City.

DF: I had one fellow, he did twenty
years in Sing Sing and he wanted his
ashes thrown over—I threw them

over Sing Sing. It's right up the
Hudson. 85

Falk says that no matter who he's
tossing, all of the ashes get equal
treatment. After all, inside each Quaker
canister lie the remains of a unique
individual. 90

DF: It's fascinating, these people
who send their ashes. Of what they
were, their stories, their lives! I
mean, uh, they worked, they loved,
they had children, they—it's, it's 95
unbelievable! And now they're, uh,
simply reduced to two and a half
pounds of the bone! In that oatmeal
box.

I feel her shaking a little 100

Often, Falk waits until he gets two or
three packages of ashes before renting a
plane and scattering them. It's a good
way to cut down on costs. But today,
Mabel is going solo. Falk opens her lid 105
for one last viewing.

DF: Here, see these are the ashes.
Now you see a couple of big ones
here. See there, feel it, feel how
heavy it is. 110
DI: Yeah, it is heavy. It looks like,
uh, just looks like sand.
DF: Yeah, it does look like sand.
Gray sand, gray.
DI: There's a little bit of, uh, Mabel 115
on my notebook here.
DF: Oh, oh, oh on here. Let me
put . . . Oh, I'm sorry.

As the statue looms larger Falk cracks
the window and begins his ritual. 120
DF: Make the most, Mabel, of what
you yet may spend until you do and

till the dust descends. Sans wine, sans song, sans singer, and sans end.

125 And like Juliet . . .

As he recites, Falk pulls the lid off Mabel, carefully flicks his wrist up, and she is sucked out of her box.

Bye bye. Bye bye. I can see her.

130 And then Mabel is gone, scattered to the wind. Although Dick Falk, who is by now a master at the art of ash sprinkling, says it is not necessarily the end for her.

DF: I try to get it up towards, uh,

135 the, uh, jet stream. And if you can get anything in the jet stream, it remains there forever. And if you have a powerful binoculars or something you can see your loved one the same

140 time, exactly to the second, every year. You see their little ashes flying by. And even if you don't see them, you look up at that second and you will have some connection with the

145 person who you loved and is now gone, and, uh, it's like a continuity of, uh, of a life!

All in all, says Dick Falk, at two hundred and fifty bucks a pop you can't really beat

150 Airplane Ashes. Still, business is not very good these days. In the early years, the heyday of his firm, Falk dumped several oatmeal boxes a week. Now he's lucky if he gets one job a month. But he

155 says that's OK. At seventy-nine years of age, Airplane Ashes is really just a hobby for him now. Falk is well aware that he can't go on flicking forever. In his Times Square office sits Dick Falk's own

160 oatmeal box, his name and a brief bio penciled in on the top. Falk has convinced a pilot friend of his to do the honors.

DF: I want to go over Forty-Second
165 Street. From one end to the other, from the docks over on, uh, Hudson to the U.N. on, uh, East River. Of course, some of it'll probably go in the block between Eighth Avenue and
170 Seventh Avenue which is a little raunchy now, but so what?

After all, when New York is your ashtray, you learn to take these sorts of things in stride.

For National Public Radio, I'm David 175 Isay.

Chapter 4 **Chained Girl**

The Marreros' small two-bedroom apartment is on the second floor of a graffiti-covered red brick building on Elliott Place in the South Bronx, one of the more dicey blocks in one of New 5 York's most drug-ravaged neighborhoods.

This afternoon, a small group of family and friends are hanging out in the living room, the same room in which fifteen- 10 year-old Linda Marrero was shackled for two months. The room is filled with too many pieces of worn, plastic-covered furniture decorated with Puerto Rican flags, plastic flowers, and small stuffed 15 animals. Visiting neighbors and friends join in a chorus of support for the parents, arrested two weeks ago for keeping their crack-addicted daughter chained to a radiator. 20

Roy Friberg: Tell me, understanding the realities of this environment, what do you do? They were forced to chain that girl.

Roy Friberg is a friend of the family's and a street drug counselor in the South Bronx.

RF: There's not a family in the world that loves their daughter any more than these people love their daughter. This was love. This was love and desperation.

Love for a fifteen-year-old daughter who, according to Maria and Eliezar Marrero, had been heading on a path towards destruction. Desperation with a social service bureaucracy that seemed unable to do anything about it.

According to the Marreros, Linda's problems began at the age of twelve. In the sixth grade, she dropped out of school and began staying out later and later at night. Soon, Linda started disappearing for days on end, returning home hungry and disheveled. Her parents say she admitted being addicted to crack. Their lives became one long search for their daughter.

This is Linda's older brother, Eliezar Jr.:

Eliezar Jr.: Be seeing my mother in the nighttime in a nightgown running down the street going after my sister.

The Marreros say they appealed to Linda's school, to the police, and to the city's child welfare agency for help, but were simply bounced back and forth in a bureaucratic nightmare. Confidentiality prevents New York City's human resource administration from commenting on the case.

The Marreros reached their breaking point this past July, after Linda had disappeared for several weeks. When she finally showed up back at the house, she was bleeding from the ears and accompanied by two men, one of whom had a gun pointed at her head. They said Linda had stolen a hundred dollars from them and they would kill her unless repaid. Maria Marrero gave them the money and made a difficult decision.

Maria Marrero: When I seen my daughter, I said, "Oh my God, maybe next time they'll kill my daughter!" You know, so I said, I told my husband, "Now please go downstairs and buy the chain. I want to put, uh, the chain on the leg." And I did it.

EM: She's my small, my small daughter. You know, fifteen years old. My baby.

The Marreros shackled their daughter Linda to the small radiator in the corner of this living room, in front of the television set, VCR, and stereo. The chain gave her enough slack to reach the bathroom and most of the other rooms in the apartment. The Marreros say that for the two months that Linda was chained, their front door was propped open, as it is today, and family friends like Roy Friberg walked in and out of the apartment with Linda's shackles in full view.

RF: I'd seen her watching TV, I'd see the chains sometimes hanging out. There was no animosity or anything, I mean it was a very comfortable situation, you know what I mean? She looked very secure, actually.

Dave Isay: Were you surprised to see her chained up.

RF: Uh, initially yeah. You know, I mean, I'd never seen it before, you know what I'm saying?

MM: She asked me for everything and I give it, everything that she wants.

DI: And, and people would come and visit her?

MM: Yeah, a lot of people would come to visit and they bring her some fruit, juice—everything that she wants.

Maria Marrero says that during the evenings if she had to go out she would bring her daughter Linda, chain and all, into one or another of her neighbors' apartments, lock her up to their radiator, and leave the keys for fear of a fire breaking out. One of those neighbors was Hermann Galliano, who lives just across the hall. He says he remembers what it was like with Linda when she was roaming the streets.

Hermann Galliano: Everybody used to be looking for her. Two or three o'clock in the morning we all gathered together at night searching for her.

DI: So everybody, everybody knew that she was chained up.

HG: Yeah, the whole building knew. Yes, it was good for her. Because everybody loved that kid. Everybody.

It was two weeks ago that an anonymous call to the city's child welfare bureau brought police streaming into the Marrero house and landed them on the front pages of the city's newspapers. The Marreros spent two nights on Rikers Island before they were released and the felony charges dropped.

The troubling case quickly disappeared from the headlines but is still very much on the minds of many in this South Bronx community, a community which seems to be growing increasingly angry with an overburdened social service system and increasingly willing to take matters into their own hands.

Again, drug counselor and family friend Roy Friberg:

RF: They wanted to care for their daughter. They tried to do the right thing for their daughter, you know what I mean? And abuse, the system has abused these people by putting them through what they're going through. And everybody has jumped all over what they did and how, well, like that's not right, you know, chaining a child blah, blah, blah. Nobody's come up with realistic alternatives for them. They're still, like, when this is over, there's no real solution to this.

Indeed, the first night that Linda was reunited with her parents she disappeared. Her father found her the next morning in a crack house. Linda remained home for the next week without chains, but at the time I was visiting the Marreros earlier this week, Linda had disappeared again for a night and a day.

Her brother Eliezar Jr. was getting
ready to go out and look for her.

180 EJ: And my mother have to chain her
up again, chain her up.

DI: Are you worried about her?

EJ: Of course I'm worried, that's my
sister. Have to worry about her.

MM: Who got my daughter now?
185 Nobody knows, only her. I want my
daughter with me.

Linda did show back up at home
several hours after my leaving the
Marreros. When she got there, her
190 parents were meeting with some
representatives of a drug treatment
program who had heard about the case.
They asked Linda whether she would be
willing to go into treatment. Linda said
195 yes. She packed up some clothes and was
driven to the program's drug treatment
center in New Hampshire where, the
family hopes, she'll remain for the next
five weeks.

200 For National Public Radio, I'm David
Isay in New York.

Chapter 5   Senior DJs

*"I don't like to wear colored shoes
in the winter." "It's a very neutral
color. And on you it looks good."*

It's Tuesday evening, party night at
5 the Pomanock Senior Center in Flushing,
Queens, and the community room is
beginning to fill up for the night's
festivities. There's nothing really out of
the ordinary about the event. In one
10 corner, club member Fritzie Levine

meticulously lays out neat rows of dietetic
cookies. The arriving seniors make their
way slowly to one of the dozen tables in
this drab cafeteria-like room, and sit
under the paper decorations of tomatoes 15
and pineapples and pears which hang
from the ceiling. But if you take one look
at tonight's entertainment, in matching
green and orange Hawaiian outfits loud
enough to deafen, you'll know why this 20
night will be different from all other
nights.

Meyer Shurr: First we have to get the
banner up before we do anything
else. 25

Estelle Shurr: I'll do the microphone.

Estelle and Meyer Shurr, senior citizen
disc jockeys—he's seventy-nine and
she's seventy-eight—are busy schlepping
in and setting up their equipment on a 30
table at the front of the room. It only
takes them a couple of minutes. They're
old hands at it now, and before you know
it the Pomanock Senior Center's
president, Rita, has grabbed the 35
microphone to warm up the crowd.

Rita: OK, may I have your attention,
how about it, give us a little, uh,
break, once in awhile we ask for it
and we always get it. Thank you. 40
OK, now tonight we're going to have
something a little different. All
kidding aside . . .

She's right. The Shurrs, white-haired
and a little pudgy, in thick eyeglasses and 45
dancing shoes, resemble no other disc
jockey pair around. It's not long before
they get the show on the road.

MS: Welcome, ladies and gentlemen.

We have music tonight for your
dancing pleasure.

It was in 1967, when the Shurrs retired,
that they first took up this trade. It was
out of the frustration they felt each time
they tried to go dancing out on the town.

MS: Frequently, the, uh, band, they
never had a good rhythm.

ES: And if they did have rhythm,
sometimes they went on and on and
didn't know when to stop.

MS: Uh, I told Estelle, "You know,
we ought to do something."

ES: So we became disc jockeys.

Early on, here, tonight, the Pomanock
seniors are proving to be a tough crowd.
No one is dancing. Some members are
tapping their fingers on the tables
impatiently or glancing at their watches.
Others motion wildly for Estelle and
Meyer to turn the volume down. The
Shurrs aren't fazed at all.

MS: As soon as they stop
socializing, they'll start dancing.

Lo and behold, Meyer has called it right.

MS: Alright, we have a, for your
Latin music we have a cha-cha
coming up.

It starts with the Rogreguezes,
Napoleon and Frieda, a dapper couple
whose elegant cha-cha is just the spark
needed to draw others to the dance floor.
Lily and Harry Kirschenblack get up,
Martha Levine grabs Tessie Katelchuk,
and before you know it the floor is
crammed with a dozen couples.

The Shurrs nod and wink at each other
knowingly. They never doubted for a
moment that things would get shaking.

The only trick now is to keep the seniors
on their feet. Meyer knows just how to
pull that off.

MS: People like to change. You
might play two foxtrots or three
foxtrots and then put in a, uh, rumba
and play a foxtrot again and then play
a cha-cha. In other words, you vary
your, uh, dances. Otherwise the
music gets monotonous.

Alright, we have a waltz coming
up there, "Fascination Waltz." Let's
make a line dance out of this here.
Everyone join in for the "Fascination
Waltz."

In this age of CDs, the Shurrs' act has a
distinctly low-tech feel to it. The music
blares from two ancient portable
speakers, which rest on either side of the
table in front of them. There's a tape
recorder and an old record player which
also serves as their amplifier. The Shurrs
say that their refusal to bow to the
pressures of the 1990s may account for
some of their success with the senior set.
You can bet that these two won't be
influenced one iota by the Billboard
charts or by MTV.

ES: I hear about Madonna and I
heard about that Live, 2 Crew
Live or something . . . wow.

MS: Yeah, that, that really wasn't
dancing. That was music
accompanying, uh, explicit, uh,
sexual scenes, which we don't get
involved with.

ES: We don't call it music.

MS: We don't even call it music.

You know, I don't go for it, uh, it rubs me the wrong way.

Step and kick. Step and kick. Step back.

130   MS: Now, there's a dance called the lambada. And it's really called the forbidden dance and, uh, people won't dance to it. I put the music on and I discontinued playing it because
135   no one would dance to the music.

    ES: I really like the lambada.

It's an hour and a half into the dance now, and the entire room, bar none, has gotten into the act. Husbands jitterbug
140   with their wives. The women well outnumber the men here, so some dance with other women, some alone, swinging an invisible partner. Even Harry Levine, sitting by himself in the corner, leans
145   forward and puckers up to put his two cents in.

    Harry Levine: [*whistles*] My sweet gypsy Rose! Yep, that's my mother-in-law.

150   Time has taken a toll on the Shurrs and their disc jockeying business. Meyer has suffered two heart attacks, one near-fatal, and Estelle is still recovering from a stroke. Recently, they've had to cut back
155   their schedule from several shows a week to maybe four or five a month. Still, they say they're a long way from packing up their albums for good.

    MS: Many a times, we, uh, we don't
160   feel right. We're suffering from our arthritis or whatever it is. And when we get down to the event, the function, and we put on the music, it's amazing how all our aches and
165   pains disappear. We really get to

enjoy the music. And we get home, we say to each other, Aren't we glad we went instead of staying home and kvetching?

    Alright, we have a ladies' choice. 170
Ladies, pick a man to dance with. Men, don't refuse the ladies when they ask you to dance. This is a ladies' choice.

DI: Are, are you tired?

MS: Uh, no, I'm not tired. No, not 175
really. We could go a couple of more hours if we have to.

ES: Oh, no. No, not a couple. One or two maybe, but no, not a couple.

    Indeed, tonight, these elder statesmen 180
of rhythm do continue to play, and the Pomanock seniors continue to dance the night away.

    For National Public Radio, I'm David Isay. 185

Chapter 6   Advance Obituaries

It's five p.m., deadline hour in the massive newsroom which has occupied the third floor of the *New York Times* building in Times Square since it opened back in 1913. This legendary room, once a 5
raucous, spittoon-filled clubhouse for cigar-smoking journalists, is quiet today, streamlined into neat rows of desks, each with a computer terminal, a telephone, and a shelf for books and clippings. 10

    In one corner of the newsroom, tucked behind the financial desk, sits the seven-person *New York Times* obituary staff. While some of these obituary writers occupy themselves with the day-to-day 15 reporting of deaths, a number devote the majority of their time to penning obituaries for people who have yet to die, people deemed worthy of a more

20 thoughtful last word in this, the paper of record, than what might be written on deadline. There's no other job like it in the entire country.

Peter Flint: This is a celebration of

25 life, of achievement, of one special person.

Peter Flint has been writing advance obituaries at the *Times* for twelve years.

PF: This is the, uh, the top drawer of

30 the files of the advance obits, uh, that I, that I've written. And it's alpha— well, I have, say, the first four or five that are being edited and that I may be called on to answer questions on.

35 And after that . . . we get to the other subjects alphabetically.

In four locked drawers are stored the hundreds of advance obituaries filed from A to Z which Peter Flint has written.

40 There are directors, actors, writers, social scientists, historians. All are well known, all are alive. Each obituary, printed on computer paper with holes running down the sides, begins with a simple lead

45 sentence. The first half gives a concise summary of the person's life, the second half reads "died (blank); he or she was (blank) years old."

The advance obituary staff call the

50 subjects of these files their "clients." For the sake of good taste, the *Times* keeps the names of these clients confidential. While Peter Flint has the hundreds of advance obituaries he's written at his

fingertips, in the morgue, or reference 55 center, of the *Times,* in two unmarked, padlocked file cabinets, are what's thought to be thousands more, although no one's ever counted.

But even with the large number of 60 advance obituaries already written, it's still a struggle to try and ensure that all major figures are covered when their time comes. So what's the trick? Peter Flint:

PF: Uh, my wife is intuitive about 65 these things. We'll be having supper and all of a sudden she'll look up and say a name. It won't be really any, any inspiration from, from, uh, radio or television or, or a book. It'll just 70 be, you know, all of a sudden the name appears. And, uh, I'll jot down the name as soon as possible and write it.

Flint's wife, Maryanne, has a knack for 75 picking clients. She blurted out Joan Crawford's name over dessert one night only two weeks before she died. She came almost as close with Hitchcock.

Once a client is chosen, the writers will 80 take anywhere from two days to a number of weeks to compose the obituary. Each writer has a personal information-gathering style.

Marilyn Burger: The fun part, I 85 think, is interviewing the subjects.

Marilyn Burger, who actor John Houseman once referred to as the "angel of death from the *New York Times*":

MB: I'll call and say, I'd like to take 90 you to lunch or I'd like to see you or I'd like an appointment. I'm from the *New York Times* and I'm doing a

story about you. Then if they say,
95 What's the story for? I say, Well, I'd
rather talk to you about it when I see
you.

Peter Flint prefers to rely on
biographies and newspaper clippings
100 when penning the obituaries of his
clients.

PF: The great majority of people
really don't like to speak to an
advance obituary writer. It makes
105 most people uneasy. And, uh, they're
almost, you know, conscious of, you
know, My golly, I'm saying
something here and it's going to
appear after I am dead. They, it
110 makes them uncomfortable, uh, some
are superstitious. I mean the fact that I
mean this man has arrived at, at your
home and, uh, I just really don't want
to think about this, uh, I mean even
115 though I know it's inevitable.

The only other inevitable involving the
obituary staff is that no one is permitted
to see his or her own obituary. Not even
Times publisher Punch Sulzberger.
120 Times have changed for the advance
obituary staff. Some of the legendary
advance writers like Alden Whitman and
Al Krebs have retired. Years ago, the
New York Times put an end to what was
125 known as the "ghoul pool," where
advance obit writers would wager on the
date that an obituary would finally make it
into print.

But there's a spirit among these
130 advance obituary writers which lives on.
A pride in ensuring that important figures
get the farewell they deserve, in

knowing that they will go out with a
flourish in the paper of record.

PF: I don't want to sound like 135
a ghoul, but it's, uh, it's a joy
to try to capture as, as, neatly
and as gracefully, as effectively
as possible, uh, the essence of
a special human being. 140
And that's, that's my obligation
and that's what I strive for.

August 13, 1982

Henry Fonda, who exemplified
for nearly half a century a man of 145
honesty and decency in more than one-
hundred films and stage plays, died early
yesterday of chronic heart disease in Los
Angeles. He was seventy-seven years old.

The actor, who retained a boyish 150
candor and a gentle but firm manner,
had long been a quintessential
American hero. His image of a
prairie Galahad was enhanced by his
clean-cut features and firm jaw, tall, 155
lean frame, loping stride, and dry wit
expressed with a distinctive middle-
western twang.

Mr. Fonda was a meticulous and
modest craftsman, dedicated and 160
intense, who thoroughly enjoyed his
profession. Mr. Fonda really lived
when he was acting and just existed
when he wasn't. He remarked, "If I
project anything of me into my roles, 165
it's maybe a man with some dignity who
tries to be honest," unquote. And then
quote, "I just want to be remembered as
a good actor" unquote.

Besides his wife and children, he 170
is survived by four grandchildren and

a sister, Harriet Warren of Omaha. The actor's wish, a spokesman said, is that there be no service and that his body be cremated. He willed his eyes to the Manhattan Eye Bank. In lieu of flowers, contributions may be made to the Henry Fonda Theater Center Memorial, care of the Omaha Community Playhouse, 6915 Cass Street, Omaha, Nebraska 68132. That's it.

For National Public Radio, I'm David Isay in New York.

Chapter 7 Diaryman

For no less than four hours each day, Reverend Robert Shields of Dayton, Washington, holes himself up in the small office off the back porch of his family's home, turns on his stereo, and types. He is surrounded by a half-dozen IBM Wheelwriters in case one of them breaks down from overuse.

Robert Shields: I can do this . . .

Shields spins around in his swivel chair.

RS: . . . and get all six typewriters without getting up. [*laughs*]

Robert Shields is seventy-five years old. He is a short, round man with an impish grin, decked out in his customary writing garb, navy blue thermal underwear and a white T-shirt. Shields was a minister and high-school English teacher in this picturesque Washington town before devoting himself to his journal.

RS: My diary is complete.

Shields is certainly not exaggerating. Over the past twenty years he has typed between three and six thousand words each day, keeping a record of everything that happens to him.

RS: The entire day is accounted for. I, I don't leave anything out. I start it in at midnight and go through the next midnight and every five minutes is, is accounted for.

12:20–12:25: I stripped to my thermals. I always do that.

12:25–12:30: I discharged urine.

12:30–12:50: I ate leftover salmon, Alaska Red salmon by Bumblebee, about seven ounces, drank ten ounces of orange juice while I read The Oxford Dictionary of Quotations.

Robert Shields types his diary in two perfect columns down sheets of 11-by-14-inch paper which he eventually binds into ledgers and stores in huge cartons, seventy-five of which are stacked to the ceiling just outside of his office.

RS: It's a, an uninhibited diary. It's, it's tell all, show all. It's spontaneous. I type it as it comes and I don't correct it and I don't edit it.

David Isay: Do you read it?

RS: No, 'cause if I read it I wouldn't have time to do anything else.

12:50–1:45: I was at the keyboard of the IBM Wheelwriter making entries for the diary. I typed diary entries since three o'clock this morning. I failed to mention, uh, that the Tri-City

Herald *weighed in this morning at one pound, eleven and a half ounces! That was the heaviest paper we have had to my knowledge. It lacked only, uh, half an ounce of being one and three-quarters pounds. Think of it.*

1:45–2:10 . . .

Robert Shields does have a background which might help to explain this undertaking. His father, John Arthur Shields, was the world's speed typing champion at the turn of the century. He would type the Gettysburg Address over and over again on a manual typewriter at a rate of 222 words per minute.

Robert Shields says that he kept a diary on and off for much of his life, but it was not until 1972 that he began to keep this minute-by-minute record.

RS: I just kept going and then I thought, Well I don't want to stop now and I kept going . . . and I don't want to stop now. And I just kept it up.

DI: Why are you doing this?

RS: It's an obsession. That's all I can say. It's an obsession. I, I don't know.

DI: What are you trying to do?

RS: I don't know. I don't really, I really can't answer that.

5:45–6:15: I read more from The Oxford Dictionary of Quotations. I ate half a dozen large Archway sugar cookies while I drank two cups of milk . . .

In his diary Robert Shields records everything he eats. He records his blood pressure and pulse at various times during the day. The temperature outside and in. Every conversation he has. Every piece of junk mail he receives. He sleeps no more than two hours at a time so that he can record his dreams. Robert Shields has also Scotch-taped a variety of his life's keepsakes into this diary, for instance, samples of his nasal hair.

RS: For DNA purposes. It might, in years to come, they might be able to figure out my genetics from having a physical artifact.

DI: What is this, in your diary?

RS: Oh, whenever we purchase anything like meat particularly, I peel the stickers off and put it in the diary, because then there's a record of, uh, how much we bought and what the price of it was.

8:35–8:40: I peeled meat labels from McQuarry to mount in the diary. Bacon is up twenty cents a pound, T-bones are terribly high. I bought them to feed Dave Isay Sunday evening. I don't know if . . .

It is somewhat disconcerting to see the extent to which this task has taken over the life of Reverend Robert Shields, chaining him to his typewriter on this endless endeavor. Shields, it seems, is so busy documenting the insignificant minutiae of his life that he has become oblivious to everything else going on around him.

DI: How does your family feel about this?

RS: Never asked them. [*laughs*]

DI: What about leaving town?

RS: I don't leave town. I haven't left town since 1985, uh, to visit my brother in Tennessee. Uh, I, I don't like to be away overnight because it gets me behind. If I travel to Walla Walla to do shopping it puts me behind in the diary. I have to take notes all the time, and get back and it takes almost a day to catch up with the notes. So I avoid going out, avoid being away.

3:05–3:30: I read the Tri-City Herald. *A sniper killed two and wounded five at El Cajon, California, for no reason at all.*

RS: It's my makeup, it's my nature, I suppose.

DI: What would it do to you if you just stopped?

RS: It'd be like stopping, turning off my life.

Reverend Robert W. Shields writes and lives in Dayton, Washington.

RS: 3:20–3:25: In the afternoon I took the readings given in the margin: humidity, 51 and a half; porch temperature, 56 degrees; porch floor temperature, 51 degrees; the study temperature, 77 degrees and the door temperature in the study, on the door jamb, 74 degrees.

Chapter 8 Passover Wine

On Rivington Street, just off Essex, in Manhattan's Lower East Side, stands an old tenement building. It's boarded up except for the bottom floor, where an ancient warped sign in Hebrew and English reads "Schapiro's House of Kosher Wines." "The wine so thick," it says, "you can almost cut it with a knife."

Customer: Mr. Schapiro, I want some wine.

Inside, the store is narrow and cramped. There are boxes everywhere. The old wooden shelves which line the wall are stacked high with bottles and jugs of "Schapiro's own." Mostly their staples: extra-heavy Concord grape and Schapiro's Malaga.

Norman Schapiro: This is the traditional Passover kiddush wine.

Norman Schapiro runs Schapiro's Wine.

NS: It's not Chateau Mouton Rothschild, but this is Chateau de Schapiro. This is my chateau.

It was Norman's grandfather, Sam, who started Schapiro's in 1899, and they've been selling their kosher vintage ever since. Even during Prohibition, when Schapiro's stayed open with a special government license to make sacramental wine.

Customer: Where are the tiny bottles?

For many years, the family did all of the winemaking here on Rivington Street, even crushing the grapes. Today the grapes are crushed at vineyards in upstate New York, but they are still trucked here to ferment in the giant oak and redwood vats in Schapiro's cavernous cellar, which takes up the entire city block. This, says longtime customer Stanley Veigh, is reason enough to bring him back to Schapiro's year after year after year.

Stanley Veigh: Bread is good to buy
straight from the bakery. That's why
wine is good to buy straight from the
winery.

For other customers, the lure of
Schapiro's is its longevity and its history.

Customer: I've been coming here
since they were open on Saturday
nights when I was a little girl and my
father used to buy a gallon and we
had it for the whole year.

Customer: It started from my mother,
God rest her soul, and father—long
time. Since I remember.

Customer: Years. Years and years.
Many, many years.

Linda Schapiro: Hello, everybody,
Happy Passover. Hi! Some of my
customers are so cute. How are you?

It's Norman Schapiro's wife, Linda, a
platinum-blonde Jewish momma, heavy
on the lipstick, who for the most part
handles the slow but steady stream of
Izzys and Esthers and Heshies and Sadies
that wander in here for their Passover
wine.

Customer: Say, there used to be a
store around here selling Jewish
horseradish.

LS: Yeah, around the corner. He still
has it.

Customer: No, not him. There's a
new, there's another place.

LS: It's very informal, you see, this
is not IBM. The office is always open,
it's Linda and Norman, you know,
you can fight with me, you can argue,
you can use the telephone. You

know, it's just not, you know, hoi
polloi.

Customer: . . . chaim. To life, to life!
L'chaim.

The most popular and lingered-at spot
is without a doubt the sampling table,
where customers can drink all of the
Schapiro's Passover wine they want out
of tiny plastic cups for free.

Customer: Yeah, this is the Malaga
and we will taste and we will make a
little barokh too. [sings] Barokh attai
Adonai . . .

A man named Ruby is here, downing
some of the more exotic new kosher
wines, like Schapiro's blanc de blanc and
Schapiro's Chablis. You couldn't drag
Sol Itskowitz away from the table if you
tried. Soon, Linda Schapiro makes her
way over and discreetly nudges me to do
some sampling of my own.

LS: Let's go. Enough of this.
Enough of this. Let's get started. So
what would you like to taste?

David Isay: What do we, what do we
have here?

LS: How about you taste my
favorite, alright?

DI: OK. Sweet.

LS: Oh, it's delicious. Come on,
David, this, this is Seder wine. Let's
cut out the, the rest of it, OK? Are
you married?

DI: No.

LS: Alright, you want to show him
the girl?

The sickly sweet grape juice taste of
Passover wine, so thick it coats the
mouth, always takes me back to my

childhood Seders. The first time I ever got drunk was on Passover wine. I was nine years old. I wept and vomited.

The next time I got drunk was also on Passover wine. I was ten years old. This time, I wept and vomited and poured out the family secrets to a table full of horrified relatives. [*sounds of a Seder dinner and of singing*]

Customer: Malaga. I need three gallons Malaga. Malaga. The heavy, the heavy, the one what you can cut with a knife. This is the one I like to have. Three gallons, please, let me have.

Times have changed here at Schapiro's. The days when crowds would mob the store from dawn until midnight, waiting to fill jugs with wine from big wooden kegs are long gone. But Schapiro's is doing a booming wholesale business supplying liquor stores from Florida to California. And Norman says that their kids, the fourth generation, are now getting ready to take over the business, although customers will miss Linda's service.

Customer: All the time, when I come here, she's right here by the cash register. She always take my money but she never overcharges.

LS: Isn't that nice?

Customer: She's always right because, you know, this is a real Schapiro lady. That's why.

Linda and Norman say that as long as there are Schapiros, there will always be Schapiro's Passover wine and there will always be a Schapiro's winery here on Manhattan's Lower East Side.

Customer: [*sings*] . . . *Schapiro's winery* . . .

LS: Hocksemeyer, thank you for being such a wonderful customer for so many years . . .

Customer: It was nice seeing you, it was a great honor and a privilege because you are a beautiful lady.

LS: Thank you very much. You're a beautiful gentleman.

For National Public Radio, I'm David Isay in New York.

Customer: *Zein gazint. Zolst zayn gezintin pesach. Un mir zoln der laybn ayor.* [You should be healthy. You should have a healthy Passover. And we should live to see another year.] All the best.

LS: Thank you very much. Thank you very much.

Customer: Bye.

Chapter 9 **The Joe Franklin Show**

On the sixth floor of an old Times Square building, Joe Franklin's cramped office looks tornado-stricken. It's permeated with the musty, Lysol-tinged smells rising from the multiplex sex emporium that occupies the floors below. There are stacks of old coffee cups, moldy half-eaten bagels, and shopping bags full of yellow newspaper clippings everywhere.

And of course there is the architect of it all, Joe Franklin, sitting at the front of the office all day, working his two rotary phones.

Joe Franklin: *Hello?*

He says he gets about a thousand calls a day from hopefuls trying to land a spot on his nightly talk show. He fields each one with that Joe Franklin flair.

JF: *Richard, I want to tell you something. You—I've got so many surprises for you. Let's talk tonight at seven o'clock, you promise? It's critical.*

Dan, I need you maniacally, pathologically.

Tell them things are concretizing, things, things are coming together, they're coagulating.

Very important, Roselyn.

Put it on the critical list, critical.

Give me a hint, give me a clue.

Tell 'em give me one more day to think.

Call back in a half-hour.

JF: Once or twice a year the phone actually explodes like a, like an artery, like a heart attack where there could be nine hundred people trying to get through on that line at one time and it actually, it actually gets a stroke, and the dial blows out. Believe it or not.

There's a lot that's hard to believe about Joe Franklin. From the fact that this is his new office—he just moved in two months ago although it looks like he's been here for decades—to the fact that he's hosted something like 28,000 episodes of his talk show over the past forty years.

In that time Joe Franklin says he's interviewed 250,000 guests. Some of them famous, like Elvis Presley, John Wayne, and Bing Crosby. Most of them not so famous.

JF: I've had, uh, dancing dentists, singing lawyers, people who played the piano standing on their heads, cab drivers who, uh, do handwriting analysis. You name it, I've had it, and if I haven't had it I'll create it.

Yeah, yeah, Fred. Look, let me play it now, give me a buzz on Friday morning, I'll make you happy. God bless you.

Joe Franklin started working in broadcasting at the age of seventeen. By the age of twenty he was hosting his own New York radio show, "Vaudeville Isn't Dead." When he was twenty-two—that was forty years ago—Joe Franklin says he invented the television talk show when a local New York station offered him a daily slot and asked him how he wanted to fill it.

JF: I said, "Well how about if I do a show of people talking nose to nose, eyeball to eyeball, face to face, toe to toe?" They said, "Joe, who's going to watch people talking? The word is television, you've got to give them vision. You've got to give them seltzer bottles, pratfalls. Got to give them movement." I defied them, and I did the first TV talk show. And, uh, look what it is today.

Announcer: *Cameras, headsets.*

Joe tapes a week's worth of programs

every Thursday afternoon at WOR-TV in Secaucus, New Jersey, on a generic-looking talk show set. In the moments just before air, Joe sits comfortably behind his host's desk, his feet not quite touching the floor, perusing some notes, paying a couple of bills, looking every bit the part of a man who's done this tens of thousands of times before.

Announcer: *Theme under, dissolve into one and cue Joe.*

JF: Once again I say good morning. I am with you wandering through memory lane, and the excitement is mounting, the excitement is mushrooming and skyrocketing and snowballing and escalating because everybody says, "Joe, is she really here, the rock and roll madam?" This lady's voice . . .

This is vintage Joe Franklin, hosting in his trademark style, giving his guests the sorts of introductions they'll never get anywhere else.

JF: *Today, one of the foremost young actresses of modern times or previous times or future times . . .*
    They are the top comedy team of their time . . .
    Everybody wants to chat with America's best-known, best-loved . . .
    We've got one of the most famed of all the plastic surgeons, a man who's all over the headlines . . .
    I, I go out of my way to give them a really, really loquacious buildup.

David Isay: How far will you go?

JF: As far as, until it gets ludicrous.

Then if it gets ludicrous, I'll still keep it in the tape.

I want to do a moment now with a man who's a very hot radio and TV guest, Mr. Richard Dardus, a most respected biotechnologist who talks about the, uh, healing powers of the ocean. For example, uh, sea cucumbers bring arthritis relief.

Joe's show is unfailingly entertaining, always offering up an incredible mix of odd characters and unpredictable situations, although Joe never makes fun of his guests and never talks down to his audience. This, he says, is the key to his longevity in the talk show field.

JF: I think I'm the last one who's organic or from the bones. I'm not plastic. I try to look in the guests' eyes, not their nose or their bellybutton.

Despite the fact that many of Joe's guests are making the one and only television appearance of their lifetime, Joe somehow seems to make them all feel comfortable. If they've got something to sell, he pushes it with gusto. If they've got a clip, he runs it. Needless to say, they are not the sorts of fancy movie trailers or music videos you're likely to find on other talk shows.

JF: Bob, set the scene please.

Guest: Yes. The name of the video is "Rock, Rock, Rock, Rock, Rock, Rock, Do the Be-Bop."

JF: And it goes exactly like this . . .

Song: *Let's go, girl, do the be-bop. Doo-wop, doo-doo-doo-wop. Kind of*

like it was at the hop. Doo-wop, doo-
doo-doo-wop. We'll make this dance
170   all shake, shake, shake . . .

Joe Franklin says that his popularity is
now at an all-time high, thanks to the
2,500 cable systems which carry his
show nationwide. Despite forty years of
175   hosting this daily program, Joe says that
he has no plans of retiring and that his
audience can look forward to thousands
and thousands of more shows just like
this one.

180   JF: Oh, you've got to be the new
Elvis, gotta be. You're a late
bloomer, right?
Guest: Yes, I am.
JF: I hope it sells a million, uh,
185   cassettes, and I've been hearing it's
doing quite well around town, right?
Guest: Yes, and thank you for saying
that.
JF: We shall return in about twenty-three
190   and a half hours. Meanwhile, have a
good everything.

At the end of the day, after hours and
hours of taping and dozens of guests, a
routine which would leave most mortals
195   gasping for air, Joe just looks
invigorated. He hops up from his host's
desk and crumples up the day's worth of
notes.

DI: So, what did you think of the
200   shows?
JF: I would say they were, uh,
superb. On a scale of one to ten,
eleven. That's my informed appraisal,
my educated assessment, that's my
205   considered opinion.

DI: Happy anniversary, Joe.
JF: Thank you. I appreciate it.

Chapter 10 Kipperman's Pawnshop and Wedding Chapel

Kipperman's Pawnshop stands out on
East Bellfort Street in Houston, a
decidedly grungy strip of fast-food joints,
beauty parlors, and liquor stores. The
building, located across the street from an   5
abandoned bowling alley, is an oasis of
color. Huge signs beckon, "We marry
you $49 No appointment necessary" and
"Hock it to me."

Ted Kipperman: One of my slogans   10
out here at this place is "When you're
in the mood to say 'I do' and you
really care, think of Kipperman's
Wedding Chapel, where love is always
in the air."   15

As you may have guessed, that is Ted
Kipperman, the mastermind of this
operation. An enormous painted portrait
of the man takes up an entire side of the
building. He looks distinctly pope-like in   20
his chaplain's outfit, a long white robe, a
red stole draped around his neck.

The inside of Kipperman's Pawnshop
is packed with the usual assortment of
hockables: TVs, VCRs, toasters, and   25
tools. Glass display cases of jewelry and
racks of guns.

TK: This is a .25 caliber pistol,
$79.95. People always kid me and
say, "This is the only place in town   30

you can get married and buy a gun all at the same time."

This is a .38 right here. Boy, that'll stop 'em.

35 The genesis of this odd combination of businesses dates back to the early 1980s. Houston had hit particularly tough economic times, and customers were hocking huge numbers of wedding rings. 40 Kipperman says that he just couldn't bring himself to melt any of them down.

TK: There's too many memories.

It became an obsession for Kipperman. His collection of surplus 45 wedding rings grew and grew and grew until one day in 1984 when Kipperman reached his breaking point.

TK: I woke up one morning in a cold sweat. "What am I going to do with 50 those wedding rings?" So God spoke to me and said, "Maybe a wedding chapel would be a good thing to put in that pawnshop."

Kipperman followed this divine 55 inspiration. He wrote away to the National Chaplain's Association and got himself ordained. Then, sparing no expense, he installed a chapel in his pawnshop. It's hard to miss. At the back 60 of the store Kipperman has built a miniature church facade complete with columns and fake stained-glass windows, the whole structure adorned with blinking Christmas lights. On an easel next to the 65 chapel entrance sits a big framed color photograph, of Kipperman.

TK: Hello, so happy to see you here. Right on time for your wedding.

Kipperman's first couple of the day has arrived. Ernest and Lucy, a 70 handsome pair who live in the neighborhood and say they were drawn to Kipperman through his "buy a ring get a free wedding" offer.

TK: Come right in here . . . 75

Kipperman leads the couple through two frosted glass doors into his wedding chapel, a small plush room with a few rows of cushioned pews.

TK: . . . stand right here . . . 80

Kipperman positions the couple at the front of the chapel and stands before them inside a seven-foot-tall wrought-iron heart threaded with plastic flowers. He hits the play button on an old cassette recorder. 85

TK: Dearly beloved, we are gathered here today to join Lucy and Ernest in marriage. They're getting married today. Why? Because they're in love with each other. 90

Ernest and Lucy have opted for Kipperman's bargain-basement wedding, passing on all of the extras he offers, like the $14.95 bouquet, a $50 value.

TK: I have a wedding gown here that 95 if they like to rent that will be $20. If they want to have a, uh, videotape of the wedding, I've got a video camera I can come in here and shoot it with them. One of my employees do 100 it for, say, $49.95. That's a good deal . . .

'til death do us part.

The ceremony is brief but heartfelt.

TK: And by the authority of the state 105 of Texas and by my authority as a chaplain and as a minister and by the still higher authority of the word of

God, I now pronounce you husband
and wife. Whom God . . .

As is wont to happen Kipperman is
overcome by the emotion of the moment.

TK: Whom God has joined together
let no man put asunder. Ernest, you
may now kiss the bride. [*kiss*]

Well, congratulations. I have Mr.
and Mrs. Ernest and Lucy Duran.
Thank you very much for letting me
officiate. Thank you, Mrs. Duran.
Now stand right there and . . .

One of Kipperman's clerks, Karl
Davis, sits at the chapel's Baldwin
organ—which, incidentally, can be
purchased for a mere $200—and plays.
In keeping with tradition Ted Kipperman
poses the newlyweds Ernest and Lucy for
a complimentary Polaroid. They toast
empty plastic champagne glasses in front
of a fake, albeit realistic looking,
wedding cake.

TK: I have to change the cake out
about every, about every four or five
months because people try to eat the
cake.

David Isay: Have you ever had
anyone actually get married and then
come in later and hock their wedding
ring?

TK: Well, once in a while they come
in when they get down on their luck,
you know. But most people, they
pick their wedding rings up after they
pawn 'em. Once in a while they
come in and tell me they don't want
their wedding rings anymore 'cause
they're, they think going to get a divorce
and do I do annulments, and I say, "No, I
don't do annulments. My weddings
are always for better or for worse."

No sooner have the newlywed Durans
departed than Rose Martinez shows up at
the pawnshop. She is here without her
betrothed, a man named Michael Smith,
who, she explains, is currently locked up
at the state's maximum-security
penitentiary. He's been there for eight
years. Rose and Michael have decided
that now is as good a time as any to tie
the knot. By telephone.

Rose Martinez: I guess we don't
want to lose each other, but, um, by
the time he comes out he'll be fifty-
some years old and I'll be fifty-some
years old, but I love him. I love him
very much and he loves me, too. So, I
guess that's what counts.

A wedding by proxy. Kipperman
knows the routine well. Rose has brought
with her a marriage license and the
prison's phone number. That is all
Kipperman needs to join the two in holy
matrimony. Unfortunately, there's no
telephone in the chapel so the ceremony
takes place out front.

TK: We'll have to do this one across
the counter.

RM: It don't matter as long that I'm
married to the man I really love.

TK: Hello, is this the, the East— the
Eastham Unit? Is Warden Morton
there?

As it turns out the groom is
unreachable, so Ted Kipperman has the
prison chaplain stand in for Michael
Smith at the penitentiary. And on this

end, who to stand in and exchange rings with the bride? Well, I do the honors.

190 TK: Dearly beloved, we are gathered here today to join Michael and Rosario in marriage. They're getting married . . .

I have to admit we were both a little nervous, but Kipperman, with his sugary smile and sure-footed execution of the

195 ceremony, puts us right at ease.

TK: Rosario, do you take, uh, Michael to be your lawful wedded husband? To live with him according to God's holy ordinances?

200 RM: I do.

TK: And, uh, we have a stand-in for the, the groom. Mr. David Isay, you do vow to take good care of her and do everything according to God's

205 holy ordinances? You say "I do."

DI: I do.

TK: Well, then by the authority of the state of Texas and by my authority as a chaplain I now pronounce you

210 husband and wife. Whom God has joined together let no man put asunder. Congratulations. Congratulations, Mrs. Smith.

And so another couple is joined in

215 matrimony. Just add them to the long list of satisfied customers who have found love at this most unlikely locale, Kipperman's Pawnshop and Wedding Chapel in Houston, Texas.

220 For National Public Radio, I'm David Isay.

RM: I appreciate it a whole lot. If my husband was here, he would thank you, too.

TK: There's more than one way to skin a cat. 225

Chapter 11 Woolworth's Lunch Counter

The luncheonette at Woolworth's in downtown Greensboro takes up the back corner of the store. A straight counter runs along one wall, a series of horseshoe-shaped counters along the 5 other. It is lunch time, and the place is packed. Customers sit shoulder to shoulder on swivel chairs. Behind one of the U-shaped counters stands a woman at a chopping board. She works 10 quickly—making sandwiches, slicing tomatoes. There is a serious, no-nonsense air about her. She rarely looks up.

Geneva Tisdale: I put myself in my 15 work. Always have.

Geneva Tisdale has worked at this lunch counter now for more than four decades.

GT: I started off as a fountain girl. 20

Geneva Tisdale was nineteen years old when the luncheonette manager gave her a job here.

GT: If she needed a glass washer, I washed glasses. If the sandwich- 25 board girl quit, she put me on the sandwich board, so I been around.

Geneva Tisdale was around in the days when African-Americans were allowed to cook, clean, and wash dishes here, but 30 weren't allowed to serve food. All of the waitresses and all of the customers were white. There were no signs prohibiting African-Americans from eating at the lunch counter, she says—everyone just knew.

The policy went unchallenged until February 1, 1960, when four freshmen from the Agricultural and Technical College of North Carolina—Franklin McCain, David Richmond, Ezell Blair Jr., and Joseph McNeil—sat down at this counter. Geneva Tisdale was working that day.

GT: At first I thought—I said it was somebody being funny. I remember passing, and, uh, I saw them sitting there, and I kept walking. But then every time somebody would pass by them, they would ask if they could be served. They wanted, uh, asked for a piece of pie and a cup of coffee. And, uh, everybody passed by them and just told them that they couldn't serve them. So that made me kind of nervous, so now I went on back to the back and I stayed back there.

At the time, Geneva Tisdale was pregnant with her third child and was sent home to wait out the sit-ins.

The protests grew quickly. On the second day there were twenty-eight students sitting at the counter, on the third there were sixty, occupying all of the luncheonette seats all day. By the sixth day, there were one thousand demonstrators in this Woolworth's. The management decided to close the counter down. It reopened two weeks later, still segregated. Woolworth's and the students negotiated for five months until the store finally announced in July that there would soon be a change in policy.

Geneva Tisdale remembers that she and two of her coworkers in the kitchen were chosen to be the first African-Americans to eat at this lunch counter. On July 25th, 1960, Geneva Tisdale was told to come to work in her uniform but to bring along a change of clothes. It was around noon, she says, that the luncheonette manager came over and told her and her coworkers what to do.

GT: She said, "Now you all go up, get dressed, walk around in the store like you a customer shopping." She said, "Have you a big bag and all." She said, "Walk around like you shopping, then come on over to the counter." And she told us where to sit. So we all did. She said, "Now, if you don't want your pictures in the paper, order something that you can eat real quick. 'Cause when, when the word gets out," she said, "the newspaper, uh, people will be in here."

I ordered a egg salad sandwich, and I swallowed it. It took me about five minutes, I'm sure. No longer than, no more than ten. And when we finished we got up and left. She said, "Go back upstairs, change back into your uniform, come back down and go to work, and let's see what happens." So we done that, and sure enough, it wasn't long before the photographer and all was in, and people started crowding in, and they didn't know it was us. [*laughs*] We were the first.

That was more than thirty years ago, and Geneva Tisdale says that she has not had a meal at this Woolworth's counter
115 since then. It was her wish, she says, to one day retire and come back with her granddaughter to eat.

GT: Just sit at the counter and be served! That's what I was hoping
120 for.

But early last week, the store manager informed her that the Woolworth's lunch counter would be closing today. Geneva Tisdale says that she is still in shock.
125 She'll miss working here but knows that her job is far from perfect. After more than forty-two continuous years of hard work behind this counter, after more than forty-two years of dedicated service to the
130 F. W. Woolworth Company, her hourly wage?

GT: $5.50 . . . $5.50.

This salary, Geneva Tisdale says, speaks to what has not changed since
135 four young men occupied this historic lunch counter in a watershed moment of the Civil Rights Movement thirty-three years ago.

GT: I feel like, sometimes, if a white
140 person had this job, that person would get paid more than me—just because the color of the skin.

The Woolworth's lunch counter in Greensboro, North Carolina, closed down
145 this afternoon for the last time. On Monday, Geneva Tisdale will be moved out onto the floor of the store and will work there until that closes in early January.

Chapter 12 Cynical Santa

It's early in the morning at Santa Central, an auditorium and the headquarters of the Volunteers of America, New York's largest supplier of Santas. Several dozen bedraggled-looking men slowly wander 5 in and pull their red suits off the long racks which sit on the room's stage. For eighty years now, Volunteers of America has been placing down-on-their-luck Santas on the streets of midtown Manhattan to 10 raise money for charity. In one corner of the room sits a thin, mustached, half-dressed Santa, hunched intently over the day's *Racing Form*. His graying hair is cut short, he's missing a front tooth, and 15 his face furrows deeply each time he frowns, which he does a lot as he suits up for the day's work.

Cynical Santa: Extra cap. Extra Belt. Safety pins. 20

This is Santa Sirwinski. Not your typical Kris Kringle, he prefers to be known as Cynical Santa. At 8:15 precisely, he's out the door.

Santa: See ya later. 25

CS: Maybe.

Santa: See you down the road.

CS: [*grunts*]

And, just a short bus ride later, he's on the job, ringing a brass bell, standing next 30 to his red chimney donation box right smack in front of Rockefeller Plaza. It's not hard to pick out Cynical Santa from all of the others. He's the one with the tobacco-stained white beard pulled down 35 under his chin, a filterless Camel dangling from his lips.

Child: Show me some magic.
Whooto, whooto.

40 CS: I'm just me. Santa Claus's
helper. That's all.
Child: Wiggle your nose and make,
um, powder come out.
CS: I'm not here to entertain people.
45 Child: Why it's not snowin'?
This is the seventh year that Cynical
Santa has worked the streets of
Manhattan with his distinctive style and
unique Santa philosophy.
50 CS: I don't believe in miracles and,
uh, fate and hope and all
that . . . praying for things and all that
other crap that, you know, a lot of
people try to push down on holidays.
55 Things just don't work that way. Not
in real life.
Santa Sirwinski should know. He's
had his fair share of hard knocks: ten
years of living on the streets of New
60 York, bouts with alcohol. Today he lives
in a Volunteers of America residence hall
and works occasionally as a welder.
Except, of course, during Christmas,
when he's paid 35 bucks plus 15 percent
65 of the donations in his chimney over
$100 each day.
Child: Santa, hi, Santa.
CS: Hi, Merry Christmas.
Mother: Uh-uh. No, don't pull his
70 beard.
It's the mornings which are the most
trying time of day for Santa Sirwinski as
he's mobbed by the thousands of eager
schoolchildren unloading from buses for
75 a tour of Rockefeller Plaza. Some shake

his hand. Some stare up at him gaping-
mouthed and silent. Others talk.
Child: Hey, you're not Santa.
Anyway, Santa doesn't smoke.
CS: Life is full of disappointments, 80
and everybody don't live happily ever
after.
Bells are ringing. Children sing, children sing.
Merry, Merry Christmas . . .
Worst of all, says Santa Sirwinski, are 85
those who serenade.
Happy New Year. Happy New
Year.
CS: You can't say, "Look, take a
walk," you know, "Get the hell out of 90
here." You know, I'm supposed to be
Santa Claus or Santa Claus's helper;
the spirit of Christmas and all
that . . . garbage.
Have a happy New Year. 95
CS: Alright, thank you, children. I
gotta go over to my chimney. I gotta
go over to my chimney.
Eddie Sirwinski says he's never taken the
etiquette lessons taught in Santa School 100
too seriously. This is a required day of
classes for all Santas at the beginning of
each season. There the men are taught
how to ring their bells, be jolly, "ho, ho,
ho." 105
CS: You know, to hell with the ho,
ho, ho's, you know.
They're taught how to say "Merry
Christmas" in a dozen languages and to
excuse themselves when they have to go 110
to the bathroom by explaining to the kids
that it's time to go feed the reindeer.
CS: I just say I gotta go pee. That's
all.

But, believe it or not, despite his unorthodox methods, Cynical Santa Sirwinski is the all-time greatest money maker in the history of the Volunteers of America. Last week he pulled in a record $400 in donations on a single day.

CS: Think about it—New Yorkers are cynical people. You know, they kind of know that I'm not a bullshit artist, you know.

Adult: If I give you a buck, will you put your mustache back on and let me take a picture?

CS: Let me take that cigarette first.

As a seven-year veteran of the Santa business, Sirwinski is full of cynical memories. There are the countless times he's been kicked and sworn at and spit on. There are the stories of his fellow Santas, like the tipsy one who accidentally fell through the windows of Bloomingdales. Or the Santa who, desperate for cash, took off his suit and sold it on the Bowery for $10.

Adult: Yo, Santa. What's happening?

CS: Nothing to it.

It's evening now at Rockefeller Plaza, and Santa Sirwinski has been working for about twelve hours. Things are not looking rosy. Donations have been coming in slowly all day. Relief Santa Smith, who was supposed to give Sirwinski a break every two or three hours, has disappeared. It's getting colder and colder. But that doesn't faze Sirwinski a bit. It would take a lot more than that to dampen this Cynical Santa's special Christmas spirit.

CS: Hi, Merry Christmas, Merry Christmas.

Child: Put that on.

CS: Nah. It's uncomfortable and it's itching me. It's just a lot of bull, anyway.

David Isay: Santa Sirwinski, do you have any sort of final Christmas message to leave with us?

CS: Everybody dies. Hi, sweetheart, throw it in the box . . . everybody dies, you know. And you wonder, what the hell? You know, what's it all about? I do.

For National Public Radio, I'm David Isay.

DI: Merry Christmas, Santa.

CS: Merry Christmas, Happy Hanukkah, whatever . . .